Mum must have been listening [...] door open before I could get out my key. She was red in the face.

'Where on earth have you been?'

'I went for a walk.'

'But it's nearly ten! I've been frantic! When I rang the Robinsons and found you weren't there . . .'

Dad loomed in the passage. 'Why didn't you let us know?'

'Sorry sorry sorry. I didn't have any money for the phone.'

'What do you want to eat?' asked Mum as if it was the last straw, pushing past us both into the kitchen.

'Nothing. I'm not hungry. I'm going to bed.'

'I'll bring you up a drink.'

I stopped on the stairs and glared over the bannisters. 'I don't want a drink.'

'Don't you talk to your mother like that,' said Dad unexpectedly.

'Leave me alone then, will you?'

Also by Josephine Poole:

The Loving Ghosts
Angel

Josephine Poole

THIS IS ME
SPEAKING

RED FOX

A Red Fox Book
Published by Random Century Children's Books
20 Vauxhall Bridge Road, London SW1V 2SA

A division of the Random Century Group
London Melbourne Sydney Auckland
Johannesburg and agencies throughout the world

First published by Hutchinson Children's Books 1990

Red Fox edition 1991

Printed and bound in Great Britain by
Cox & Wyman Ltd, Reading, Berkshire

ISBN 0 09 974030 3

To Caroline with love

There is a star
Shining afar,
Beckoning you, my friend.
Life is a climb most of the time,
But you'll get there, in the end.
Whenever you fall – and falls will come –
Whatever the trouble and pain,
Pick yourself up
Dust yourself down
And start all over again.

1

This is me, in front of the glass, one hour before the party.

Brown hair, dead straight, cut short and brushed to the side with ozone-friendly spray. Straight line of eyebrows needing to be plucked apart. Straight nose, determined mouth, strong jawline. Smallish grey-blue eyes with pale brown lashes.

My hand unscrewing the tube of mascara looks competent, more scientific than arty. I enlarge my little eyes, then paint my lips pale pink, and dab round my neck with perfume. Still in my bra and slip, I get up, stand back from the glass, eye myself critically from all angles.

I have been growing into this face, this body for over fifteen years, but there's still childishness in the way I study my reflection, as if an adult me is only a projection, something to try on, to wear in an experimental way at a party. As things turn out, I shan't see myself like this, ever again.

My dress, size fourteen, lies on the bed; in a minute I shall put it on.

This is the first and last time I shall wear it.

2

Bella's birthday party was one of the highlights of the Christmas term. She always invited everyone in our class, and this year she had announced that she was including all her unmarried uncles, brothers and male cousins, who work in the family takeaway pizza chain, and she'd told any of us with brothers or boyfriends to bring them along. I have only one sister, older and married, and a couple of boys I invited at the last minute were already busy, so it was in an unattached state that Dad dropped me at the end of the drive and said he'd collect me when the party finished at twelve-thirty.

A double row of smoky torches led from the gate up to the house, which was itself a blaze of light. The gravel crunched frostily under my feet as I walked self-consciously to the front door. It was ajar and in I went. The honey and cream decor exactly matched the labrador puppy which had been the centre of attraction last year, but was now presumably shut up somewhere. A loud, warm noise of socializing came from the room on the left, but I stood at a loss for a minute in the empty hall – only for a minute, because Bella, true to the instincts of a born hostess, bobbed out in a strapless black dress most of us couldn't have afforded.

'Hi! Good to see you – oh! Thanks!' as I handed over her present. 'I'll take your coat.'

'That's okay, where shall I put it?'

'Sure? Upstairs, first left, the light's on. Thanks, Liz!' And she bustled on down the hall.

There was a double bed piled with coats, and I laid mine on top. There was a bathroom en suite so I took the opportunity, washed my hands, glanced in the glass. Then I went downstairs and joined the party, adding myself to the group just inside the door, most of whom I knew. This was when I needed my friend, Ann Robinson, but she was ill with flu. So I smiled round, and soon someone gave me a glass of hot punch, which was useful for warming the fingers. I drank it quickly to launch myself into party mood. It was a cider cup, heavily spiced, with sliced apples floating on the top.

The two large rooms on this side of the house had been opened into one by pushing back the screen that separated them, but even so space was crowded, and for once (unusual at girls' parties) there were plenty of men. Bella's Italian relatives were mingling with the Brits, exotic creatures from a warmer clime, even if they had got no nearer to their mother country than watching 'A Room with a View'. Not all the tribe had done as well as the Rossis, who swanned home every year, and always invited rich and poor alike. We girls already knew which of us were going to be singled out for special notice, and I did not expect to be one of the chosen. I am too tall for Italian taste, and my figure is more sporting than magnetic.

I took another glass of punch from a passing tray; they were handing what Bella calls canopies as well, but not within reach. The proper food was laid out on a table covered with a white cloth, at the far end of the room – sweet and savoury dishes in lavish amounts, interspersed with vases of white freesias, and Bella's cake the centrepiece, like a model for St Paul's, beautifully reflected in the plate glass that opens in summer on to the patio and swimming pool. I could see Mrs Rossi hovering about the edible offerings, a prototype of how Bella will look in twenty-five years or so – rather overweight, rather made-up, rather high-heeled, rather low-cut – but kind from the heart, always a smile and a meal for a friend. The genes could be worse.

On the subject of genes – there is absolutely no possibility of my turning out like Mum. She is basically a charity person, warm, pretty, indefatigable voluntary worker, seller of flags, distributor of pamphlets – lit, no matter who cries for help, by her personal glow of caring concern. I fear I am a bit cold-blooded about that sort of thing.

Perhaps just cold-blooded. I suddenly wished I was different – little, curvy, vivacious – as I watched the couples forming and the dancing beginning. Maybe one day it'll be possible, complete physical transformation with pills or microchip. Somebody said, 'What's the joke?'

When I realized they were talking to me I said, 'I was wondering how it feels to be Italian.'

'Why should it feel any different?' Severity in the tone, as if I was casting aspersions on my hosts.

But I must find an Italian. I long to dance, my cold blood is tingling, my naturally pale cheeks are pink now and my little eyes sparkling, my foot (size seven) tapping out the beat. What am I doing in this hen group of obvious wallflowers who are animatedly discussing a film I haven't seen? In a pause, somebody thinks of asking me how Ann is, which is annoying; I don't want to look as if I'm missing her. I've finished my drink. I crunch the apple slices, picking them out with my fingers. The room throbs with music, the floor pulses with dancing feet. 'I'm drinking rather a lot of this,' I say, taking a third glass. To me my voice sounds unnaturally loud, but the person handing the tray only smiles and moves on. Is it a fact that drink goes more quickly to your head if you keep still? Are the effects of alcohol mitigated by dancing and chat? One of our wallflowers is picked and I step quickly into the lucky space. Just after that the sixteen candles on Bella's cake go up together in a sheet of flame, and we all sing 'Happy Birthday to You', and finding with surprise that my glass is empty again I help myself to a fourth to drink the toast.

I have an idea I am smiling, though my features aren't quite under control. There is this not unpleasant numbness in my lips and nose, on top of the warm fumes that are buoying me up. I have the feeling that I could speak strong

4

original words out of my detached lips, and I wish I was wearing Chrissie's flounced emerald skirt, with bare feet and a bolero. It is a time for dancing on that table so heavily cluttered with plates of savoury sweets. Yes I could enjoy this party, in fact it is an exceedingly good party, probably the best I have ever been at. My nostrils pinch as I draw in a breath, for what leap forward I shall never know, because quite suddenly that roomful of people tilts and I have to lurch to keep my balance. I grab an arm – it is Mr Rossi's; he is fat and his hair is prematurely white, and he has covered himself with aftershave and body lotion. He presses me to his strong paunch and we jig our way between the couples, me staring past his boyish white quiff with the suspicion that my eyes aren't focusing properly. He doesn't speak at all (surely he must know English) but he spins expertly and if sometimes I catch his pointed toes with my Anglo-Saxon feet, he doesn't complain. He gives me a glass of punch and leaves me with an uncle, and I have to drink up quickly because we are off again, this time at a gallop, disrupting more conventional couples, the tall thin uncle dropping kisses on my hair, and my lips stretched in a witless grin. More punch and on with the dance, Elizabeth solo accompanying herself on the vocal chords, which may be a shock for those in my class who class me as a sober swot, while following with intricate footwork a Latin American rhythm. Glorious party! I feel perfectly relaxed and happy and utterly myself.

It comes into my mind that food would be a good thing. Pretty soon I know that food is a must. I move in that direction, an erratic progress, what with the milling throng and the slight dislocation between my intention and my feet. The tide of music breaks in my ears. A sudden blackness hits me between the eyes – with a hideous undertow of nausea. Panic! I'm going to be sick! It ebbs, leaving me struggling for a door. I lurch through it into the kitchen. Mrs Rossi is taking a tray of little hot things out of the oven. She

5

rises and falls with the tidal linoleum. Her hands (in oven gloves the shape of scarlet hearts) full, she sizes me up instantly, jerks her rinsed curls in the direction of the passage. 'Out there, dear. First on the left, that's your nearest.' And I fall out of the room. I miss the first left, fall into the broom cupboard, extricate myself with rough gestures. Across the heaving hall, the stairs rear like an upholstered cliff which has to be scaled on all fours.

The bathroom light is blinding. I switch it off, direct myself at the bed, creep in under the coats. Thrusting away the pillows I lie flat, surging, floating on the micro-sprung interior which vibrates to the merry thump of the dance. The window reflects orange lights on the ceiling, which shift as the night wind moves the branches of the tree outside. I lie very still and shut my eyes.

It comes to me after a while that I am no longer alone in the room. Somebody is feeling through the coats, probably looking for her bag. I'm unseen at first; then a hand meets my leg, and someone mutters something I don't catch. I make words – I don't know what – at least I seem to speak but there is no response. I inch open my eyes for long enough to spot a male silhouette against the window. Silence.

He is sympathetic, he takes my hand. Moaning I return the pressure of his fingers. He strokes my wrist, my arm, the hollow of my elbow. The bed moves under me and he is there pushing his arm behind my neck. I turn to face him, wanting comfort; he is warm, kind, gently stroking my hair. He starts massaging my shoulders, my spine, a warm and lovely feeling wakes in my body begins to carry me away I press tightly against him not wanting him to stop he laughs in my ear an intimate laugh for the two of us

warm and lovely learning to ride the giddy waves

but dear God *what's happening* I wanted this but I don't want *this* I try to swear at him but the words won't come with his lips crushing my lips however I twist my head it's something new for me to be at somebody's mercy I can't

6

dislodge him though he's a lightweight ordinarily I'd have him on the floor in a minute

my dress zips up the back and after a fumble he doesn't bother with it a trickle of tears meets the sweat on my face oh God oh God come somebody *why doesn't somebody come*

whose breath is that piston noise in my ears *this can't*

screaming small like in a nightmare his hand cramming my mouth his fist between my thighs

eyes stretched fixed on the nightmare pattern shifting orange orange shifting

bruising tearing me apart pain that is pain without properly connecting it can't it can't it has to be happening to someone else

utter blackness of a faint or sleep

Mrs Rossi woke me when she turned on the light. 'Elizabet?' I opened my eyes. 'All right now, dear? Your daddy's downstairs. Better wash your face a minute.' While she ran the tap I emerged, sick and shaky, from the bed. My skirt was rucked up and I pulled it down. My tights were in ribbons and I pulled them off and stuffed them into my pocket. She turned to look at me. 'Have you got a head? Do you want a Dispring? That's right, you'll feel better for a wash. Is this your coat?' I tottered out on to the landing and picked my way down the brightly lit stairs. Dad was waiting at the bottom. I suddenly wished – how intensely wished – that it was last year with the outing and the puppy.

'Thanks for the party, Mrs Rossi.'

'Lovely to see you, darling. Take care.' To Dad, 'Just a spot too much cup. She'll be right as rain in the morning.' From Bella, radiant on the crest of a wonderful evening, ''Bye, Liz! Thanks for the chocs!'

We walked down the drive. The car felt cold. We drove silently home through the empty, black and orange streets. Dad said, as he opened the door for me to enter the house in front of him, 'I hope you didn't disgrace yourself.'

I didn't bother to reply, or thank him for collecting me. It was late, but not too late to throw all my clothes into the wash, and have a shower. After, I lay awake for a while in the narrow bed that had always been mine.

It must have been some sort of hysterical experience caused by drinking too much. *It must have been.* Mrs Rossi was no fool, and she had heaps of kids; she'd have known about it as soon as she came into the bedroom otherwise. Or all those girls who would have wanted to make up during the evening, or use the bathroom – it was just inconceivable that they had gone in and out and no one had noticed anything!

I wrapped my legs in my dressing gown to stop them from trembling, pulled up the quilt, and turned on my side to sleep. It was simply not possible that any of *that* could have happened.

3

I woke next morning when Dad blasted off to the golf club, and knew from that what time it was, without having to look at my watch. The house was silent but for the faint hum of machinery in the kitchen behind closed doors. I knew that Mum was trying not to disturb me; she has this little job which means that she has to do all the cleaning on Sundays, but today she was evidently respecting my hangover. In fact I felt well, completely restored by sleep, and although I found that I was stiff and sore in parts when I got out of bed, I did remember falling into the Rossi broom cupboard. I went downstairs in my dressing gown and slippers. She was making pasta at the kitchen table, wearing her hessian apron with the charity logo, her hair tied back with a Boots elastic. She isn't very tall, I'd outgrown her at thirteen. I often have a disconcerting feeling that she is years younger than I am. It is this question of ideals.

'Good party, Pidge?'

'Okay.' My orange juice and muesli were waiting at the other end of the table. I sat down. 'Very good, in fact. Dancing.'

'That's nice. Meet anybody nice?'

'Heaps of nice people.'

A pause. 'Dad said you overdid the drink.'

'I'd have been okay with some food. There were just so many there. But it was good fun.'

'You weren't sick?'

'God, no! I started feeling bad, so I went upstairs and lay down.' I tipped up the carton. 'Is there any more juice?'

She passed it from the fridge. 'What were you drinking?'

'Cider cup.'

'It could have been laced with brandy.'

'No way! Not at the Rossis'.'

She sprinkled some flour over the dough. I looked at the mound and a thought struck me. 'Are Chrissie and Pete coming over?'

'You'd forgotten? You promised to make a cheesecake.'

'I can't, I've got too much work. Ring Chrissie, tell her to bring one. She's got a free morning.' My mouth was full of muesli, and crumbs flew from my lips while I was speaking. Mum glanced at me quickly, annoyed. But I knew she wouldn't pick on my manners, or force me to make the pudding. And I had genuinely forgotten that my sister was coming, with her husband, the world's number one wimp.

I didn't talk any more about the party, or wash up – there wasn't much anyhow. I went upstairs and dressed, and read through some history. My room was comfortable for homework, with shelves, cupboard and desk units all screwed together and varnished by Dad; he had double-glazed the window, and put in a shower compartment, so that I had virtually my own little flat within the house. Chrissie had never done much at school, so he was doubly proud of me. Now I was studying for mock GCSEs after Christmas, going over the work I knew perfectly well already. At that time I was often amazed because moderately intelligent people seemed to make such a difficulty of it.

I was roused from my book by Fletcher, Chrissie and Pete's dog, who scratching at the imperfectly shut door, came in and put his chin on my knee. I preferred him to his owners. I stroked his head and we went down to lunch together. Dad arrived late with a red face, having had one or two at the club, and he was annoyed because there was vegetable lasagne for Sunday lunch, even though Mum had grilled pork chops for him and me. Chrissie stopped eating meat when she met Pete, so Mum felt more confident about her own fads, and she kept up a light conversation with the young couple. Pudding was tinned creamed rice and frozen strawberries. While we were licking our spoons, Pete said that he and Chrissie had decided that they would take Fletcher for a nice long walk that afternoon, because it was such a lovely day. Bracing myself against the earthquake shocks following this globe-shattering announcement, I noticed that he was right: it *was* a lovely day, the sunshine glowing in Mum's autumn leaf arrangement, and sparkling on the clean bits of glass and silver.

'Coming, Pidge?' he went on, bravely using my silly family name, turning in my direction. No thanks, Pete, you don't tempt me at all, and what my sister saw in you I shall never know, for she used to be a beautiful animated blonde with many boyfriends.

'I thought I'd go over to Ann's this afternoon.'

'Don't get flu,' warned Mum.

'She can't *still* be infectious,' I told her scornfully.

She looked at Pete. 'I'll come. It'll be perfect, along the river,' She is just such a nice person. Quite often I find it unbearable.

Dad said he would clean the car.

I made instant coffee for him and me, and while the kettle was boiling I watched the three set off down the road. Chrissie of the elegant figure looked shapeless in a brown woolly coat and the boots Pete gave her last year, with his scarf round her head. She'd taken to wearing specs and hardly ever removed them. Mum was walking twice as fast beside her in her navy duffel coat and paisley-pattern shawl; and at a little distance Pete's jaunty figure in jacket and cords darted and paused at the whim of the dog, whose lead he grasped in one chapped hand. Chrissie and Mum were already deep in conversation. I watched some sport with Dad while we had our coffee, and then I left him to the television, and wrapped myself up and went out.

Ann and I met at nursery school, and had been friends ever since. Basically we were the same type – extrovert, pretty good at games without being particularly competitive, A-stream material without having to work ourselves into the ground. We didn't go in for girly confidences, but even so I was closer to her than I was to anyone else. We were both ambitious. She veered towards the arts and wanted to go into publishing; I wanted to be a vet.

The corner shop was open and I bought her a box of fruit jellies. That was another thing that used to surprise me at that time – because I'm trying to remember as truthfully as possible what I was like in those days. People at school were always running out of cash and having to borrow from each other, but I never did. Nor did Ann, though I suspect (not having laid our coins on the table) that she had more to spend.

She lived in the older part of the suburb, where the houses were bigger than ours. The front garden was paved and covered with dead leaves from the cherry tree; I'd fallen down more than once on their path. Her mother opened the door. She worked from home, she was an editor of some sort, and Mr Robinson was in advertising. I liked their house, which was somehow scruffier inside than ours – not dirty, but used. They hadn't had a new carpet for as long as I'd known them, the front room was full of books but the sofa and chairs didn't match, and though they had TV it didn't stick out as the sole source of entertainment, or take up much of their time. There were things my mother thought important that Mrs Robinson didn't know or care about. The result was civilized in a homely and relaxed way that I liked a lot, and I visited Ann much more often than she came to me.

'Hello, Pidge!' Mrs Robinson was the only person outside our family who called me by my nickname. 'I've managed to nail her to the bed but she's bored out of her mind. She'll be very pleased to see you.'

Ann heard me and called and started to cough, so I hung my coat over the banisters and went up. She was propped against several pillows, looking wan, her curly hair lank and dark shadows round her eyes. The duvet was covered with reading matter, including the inevitable revision books. It all looked fairly uncomfortable. I gave her the sweets. 'D'you mind if I open a window? It's like an oven in here!'

'Go ahead! I can't get warm so it won't make any difference.'

So we chatted, mostly about school, because she'd missed several days, and after a while her mother came up with mugs of coffee, and clucked and shut the window. But all the while I was sidestepping, so to speak, the real reason for my visit. For I wanted to talk to her in confidence about that episode at Bella's; I wanted to know whether she thought it was possible to have that sort of hysterical experience. I just wanted her opinion, because I couldn't help feeling uneasy about it. It was like a shadow in the depths of my mind. I expected her to ask me about the party, but she didn't, so at last I had to broach the subject.

'It was good fun at Bella's.'

'Oh, the party! I'd forgotten about it. You went, did you? Who did you take?'

'Nobody, but it didn't matter.'

'Brilliant food as usual?'

'Probably, but I didn't manage to grab any. I was dancing most of the time.'

'The belly of the ball as you might say.'

I laughed though I didn't think it funny. 'And I got a bit drunk.'

'On cider, I bet.'

'Yes, it was, as a matter of fact.'

Ann knew all about cider cup because they'd had it last summer when they were staying with an old aunt in Wales. Her young brother had got completely legless on it, and now she launched into the full history of the family embarrassment. I stared out of the window. The golden and blue afternoon was thickening into mist as evening approached – turning into a grey advancing fog, raw and miserable. There were birds perching in the Robinsons' bare tree, scattered among the branches like leftover fruits. '— with the result that they didn't speak to us for months. Which was something to be thankful for,' Ann finished, and not expecting any reaction from me, since she had seen all along that I wasn't listening, she added, 'Go on about Bella's. Anything juicy to report?'

And then of course I knew I couldn't tell her. We weren't on the same wavelength that afternoon; it happens sometimes, between the best of friends. I described some of the outfits, and the Italian relatives. Mrs Robinson looked in again.

'My dear children, don't you want the light on? Here you are, sitting in total darkness!' She pulled the switch. 'There's a crumpet downstairs, if you like,' she added to me while Ann made sick noises.

'I ought to go back. It's getting foggy.'

'No rush. Have some tea first with Steve and me. I can easily run you home.'

But I didn't want to stay any longer, though the smell of crumpets was tempting on the stairs, and I am rather fond of Stephen, who told Ann, when he was a little boy, that he meant to marry me when he grew up. Mrs Robinson saw me out. The fog had crept right up to the garden gate. 'Are you sure you don't want me to run you home?' she asked doubtfully from the doorway.

'No thanks, I'll be fine. It's no distance.'

The nearest streetlamps were visible in a fuzz of light. Everything was moist to the touch, as if the fog melted as soon as it met anything solid. I was leaving a trail of footprints along the damp pavement. I knew the way so well, I could have walked blindfold; and yet I was surprised, in this fog, by the landmarks that appeared too suddenly, looming out of the opaque atmosphere. There were no other people about, no traffic. My steps had the beat of a suspense film.

The shop where I had bought Ann's sweets was still open. As I turned the corner into our road, I could just see our house. I could make out the farewell group on the pavement by Pete's car, and hear the goodbyes in the unnatural stillness of that evening. So I retreated, and took my time choosing a packet of mints, and while I was paying for it I heard Chrissie and Pete drive past. I came out then and went home, and Mum said, meeting me in the hall, 'Oh, what a shame! You've just missed them!'

Next day there was a drama at school. Bella and some of her group cornered me in the cloakroom; I'd thought she was looking upset, without knowing why.

'The most horrible thing happened at my party, Liz,' she said. 'Rachel had her purse nicked.'

I'd also noticed that Rachel looked as if she'd been crying. I am moderately observant, without being part of the girly gaggle that goes on between lessons. That doesn't mean that I'm on bad terms with anyone, but Ann and I keep ourselves to ourselves.

'That's awful,' I said, genuinely shocked. 'How did it happen?'

'It was in her coat pocket,' somebody said. And somebody else wondered whether I'd seen anything when I was lying down upstairs.

'Anybody could have got in. The front door was left on the catch,' said Bella. 'That's typical Mum. She's so trusting.'

Now here was my explanation! Some sneakthief had been feeling about for money in the pockets of the coats, and in my intoxicated state I'd imagined dreadful things. Unexpectedly, I felt enormously relieved. I said, 'Yes, there was someone.' This caused a sensation. 'It was a bloke – smallish and slim.'

'Would you recognize him?' asked Bella.

'No way – he was like a silhouette – a shadow.'

'I'd have screamed,' someone said. 'Why didn't you shout for help?'

'I did, but nobody heard. Of course I didn't know he was a thief. I was feeling terrible . . .'

'It was lucky you were there, all the same. It could have been worse. You must have given him a fright,' said Bella.

So we left it at that. And now the only thing I had to worry about was whether I would get flu from Ann, but I didn't; I hardly ever caught anything.

4

So it was the end of term. Ann came first in Eng., Eng. lit. and art; I was top in everything else. Our usual division of the spoils, which caused no surprise and only a formality of congratulations. 'Form Places' and the Head's pep talk were followed by the school play, in which I took the male lead. And Mum and Dad sat in the front row, and went on glowing with pride and appreciation.

All the same it's easier for them when I am mostly occupied at school, and last summer holidays had been a bit of a stretch from day one – yawn sport yawn – with friends away on holiday in exotic places. But three weeks over Christmas were easy to fill with shopping, parties and shows. I spent a day in the West End and found an Indian bazaar where I got most of my presents. We have this silly tradition at school of giving something to every person in the class, which means finding about thirty tiny gifts. Of course you get it all back, but I can do without heaps of sachets of henna rinse or minipackets of tissues or bath cubes. This year however I bought two dozen little boxes, all different and possibly hand-painted, for less than ten pounds. I was pleased, and when I got home I laid them out to admire on the kitchen table.

'What are you going to put in them?' asked Mum.

That is exactly the sort of question that underlines the differences between us. For Mum, a box is a container. It has to surround something. For me, once you fill it, it loses its potential. You have tamed it and earthed it. I like empty boxes.

'You could put sweets in them,' she suggested helpfully. She

17

looked at me, the kettle poised. 'Do you want camomile tea?'

'No thanks.'

She filled two mugs and returned to the sitting room, where her friend Doris was lying flat on the carpet because of her back problem. They used to enjoy a glass of wine but recently they had got into the herbs and special bath oils, and talked a lot about their weight. Doris would sip her tea from a bent plastic straw while Mum imbibed in the lotus position. They jogged and sold flags together.

It is more difficult to give a profile of Dad.

From the start Chrissie was an academic disappointment, and then in his opinion she squandered her physical advantages – because Chrissie really was beautiful – when she married Pete. Now Dad looked to me to fill the gaps, and this was a bit frightening, however strong my self-confidence naturally and by attainment. So I had recently adopted a challenging way of talking with him, which he quite liked. He hardly seemed to notice or care when I was rude to Mum, but oddly enough I could be rude to him as well, and he seemed almost to admire my nerve; he would give me an appreciative glance from his very dark eyes, maybe smile as if my contemptuous remarks were a proof of intellectual superiority – I was a person who even in my teens, couldn't suffer fools gladly. It isn't nice to remember all this, but I can only state, in my own defence, that important exams were looming, and there was a great deal at stake. Dad with a *shadowed* expression was not a pleasant spectacle.

In person he was about average height, active, lithe for a forty-five-year-old, with thick straight iron-grey hair and a reddish skin – the darkly suffused complexion that often goes with a quick temper, which he had. He thought himself underpaid and understretched at work, but he hadn't much in the way of qualifications, and this explained why he was so ambitious for his children. I could see that he was dogged by his failures, and he counted on me to make up for them. And that's enough. It mattered though, to all of us, because it made our lives difficult – especially mine. I knew for instance that he was jealous of the Robinsons, and yet he wanted me to go there. He wanted me to be aware of the differences between their home and my own, and to prefer theirs.

When I was younger, just starting to grow up – at that physio/psychological watershed – I had the idea that it was me that was keeping Mum and Dad together. A heroic role, and at that time I spent many hours with him in his shed, which smelt of creosote and oily rags and had a carpenter's bench made by himself to make things on, – my bedroom furniture for instance. I used to sit on a backless chair and help with measurements. But later I realized that the noises they made in their room, when I should have been asleep, were them making love, and they were happy then. They still made love with the light on.

So Christmas was upon us with its traditional feast of turkey and ham on the bone, homemade pudding and mincepies; but the gorging was marred by Chrissie and Pete, who poked at the meat with their forks and sneaked it to the dog. This maddened Dad. His mother always stays over the festive season; we don't see her much otherwise. She is little and hyperactive, with thick spectacles that make her head look like an insect's. She notices everything and has an unholy talent for putting the unmentionable into words, and when she saw Chrissie picking at her food, she said at once (thick north-country accent to get the full nosey commiseration of it), 'What's the matter, love? You're not *expect*ing, are you?'

Chrissie and Pete had been married three years, and as she only worked part-time, we assumed she was trying to get pregnant. Pete went scarlet, Chrissie left the room, Mum and Dad looked at each other. I wanted to chuck a sprout at Gran, who asked with perhaps genuine innocence, 'What's wrong? I've not dropped a brick, have I?'

When I was younger she'd made me blush for weeks by asking me whether I'd 'started'. A propos of which, I experienced a sudden exhaustion on Christmas Day, between the meat and pudding courses, and remembered that it was about due. But soon there was the excitement of the presents. I knew what I was getting from Mum and Dad, and it was as good as expected. Gran gave me pale blue gloves in a vile manmade fabric that was so stiff I couldn't bend my fingers. Chrissie really liked her oriental lampshade, and the Indian slippers fitted Pete; I couldn't imagine ever accepting him as part of our family, but I did feel more kindly towards them both that afternoon.

It was grey, raw weather, soon closing to dusk, not tempting even my fitness-freak little brother-in-law to a walk. The three of us sat at the back of the room with the dog, while Gran detailed how cleverly she had shopped for all our presents with her pension. Dad sat with his head back and his eyes shut, whether asleep or not; but Mum appeared to be listening. She had piled her hair on top of her head and looped it with Christmas decorations, for gaiety, and a talking point. It made her strangely top-heavy in the dimming room, a carnival figure; only her face was not carnival, but composed, pale and strained – the face of a Roman matron at assassination time. I felt a sudden stab of what could have been compassion, followed at once (self-defence mechanism automatically taking over) by an equally piercing rush of irritation. Why didn't she tell the old bag to shut up? Why did she sit there taking the spiel, when we all knew that Gran lived with and did the accounts for Uncle Jerry, who was (we supposed) superlatively rich and successful with his three petrol stations? ('Ee, but he works does Jerry' – one in the eye for sleeping Dad; the sort of witless comparison that was still the root, needless to point out, of his before-mentioned inadequacy problem that plagued us all.)

I sat on the floor with my arms round the dog, sensing the soft acquiescence of Chrissie and Pete, who like Mum saw Gran as a necessary evil, part of the warp and woof of family life etc. Why did we have to act out these lies, just because it was Christmas? Suddenly I longed to tear the fantasy to bits. Anyhow I was clever and tough, things were going to be different for me. I remember actually trembling that afternoon with the intensity of my feelings.

'Seen anything of Sy?' Chrissie wanted to know.

'We're going out on Friday.'

'Doing anything nice?'

'It's a celebration because he passed his driving test. I think we're going to a club.'

'Have fun.' Maybe she was regretting the clubs she used to go to. I couldn't tell from her face.

Sy was tall and short-sighted and very thin, and to Ann I laughed and called him a weed; but secretly I admired him because he was clever and went to a public school, which was why he hadn't been able to escort me to Bella's. As far as I was concerned, the highlight of the holidays was Our Evening Out. I had planned to wear my party dress, since he hadn't seen it, but when I got it out of the cupboard I found I didn't like it any more. Questionable vapours seemed to cling to it. So I bought a black mini-skirt and a kingfisher-blue top in the sales.

Later Mum said, 'He's picking you up here, isn't he?'

'Yes.'

'Don't forget to invite him in for a drink. There's plenty of sherry over from Christmas.'

'He won't want anything.'

'He might if you ask him.'

'He hardly drinks. There's no point.'

A little, icy pause. Then Mum said, 'Your father and I would like to meet him, please.' No comment from me. I could guess what was coming. 'Are you ashamed of us, Elizabeth?'

'Of course she is. She's not stupid,' said Dad.

Gran (still with us) was peering from face to face, out of her depth but wanting to put her oar in.

'Why should I be ashamed?' I said loudly. 'If I was ashamed I'd say so.' This was a lie. I don't know whether they knew it. 'Simon is shy and would prefer not to come in. However, since you insist, I'll make him. Anyway, what are you going to do if you don't like him?'

'I'm sure we will, if he's your friend.' Dear old Mum.

'In that case why bother?' I left her to reflect on her own illogicality and went upstairs to change.

I looked good in the black and turquoise, leggy and sexy. My face was still wrong but I got to work on it with Chrissie's present, a make-up outfit with brilliant colour combinations and a magnifying mirror, housed in its own little plastic trunk. I didn't come down until Sy was due. Gran was on her own in the front room. She scrutinized me, up and down, and to my rage I felt myself blushing.

'My father would have made me wash off all that warpaint, and if I'd refused he'd have done it for me. My father would have smacked my bottom if I'd worn my skirt as short as that,' she then recited, in a sing-song voice that shredded my self-control.

'Why don't you go home, you horrible little old clockwork person!'

This outburst astonished her, and she was still goggling and gulping when Sy rang the bell and I went out to the hall to open the door. My appearance surprised him, but I could see that he liked it. He helped me on with my coat. I gave Mum a shout and she emerged from the kitchen, too quickly, she'd obviously been lurking there, awaiting the summons.

'This is Sy,' I said.

He made a sort of plunge past me to shake her hand. 'Good evening, Mrs. . . .' and then there was silence.

'Can I offer you a glass of anything? Would you like a coffee?' She spoke brightly, as from behind a counter.

'No, honestly, thanks all the same—'

I cut short the embarrassment. 'Come on. 'Bye, Mum. I'll be back late, can you tell Dad to leave the key?'

And we escaped. Inside the car we burst out laughing.

'I didn't mean to be rude, but I simply couldn't remember your surname! What is it, anyway?'

'Russell. What's Sy short for?'

'Cyril. Keep laughing.'

Simon, I'd thought. How little we knew about each other, and yet I made passes at him all evening as if he was the most attractive man in the world. It was the cheapie clothes. 'I can see there's another side to you,' he said enthusiastically, pushing me round to the music. He didn't dance well. Neither did I, but dancing is like being attractive: a knack which depends on your partner. We kept getting out of step, as if we heard different rhythms. After a while I began to feel deflated.

'Let's eat,' he said. He had booked a table and he was at ease with the waiter, ordering for us both and selecting a wine. I had to admire his polish. His face too had improved since last time, he wasn't so spotty, he was wearing stylish specs and he had more to shave. But this evening he was trying out a line in heavy flirtatiousness; this sort of thing – 'I think I'm going to have to ask you for a good-night kiss!' I didn't like it much. It got worse the more he drank, and he drank most of the bottle. I had one glass, and even then, after a couple of swallows, I felt very odd – giddy, and sick. I gripped my hands together in my lap and the crisis passed. The food was good and I ate a lot.

Driving back he had difficulty in keeping to his side of the road, and he dithered over crossings and roundabouts. This made me edgy and I was glad there weren't any police about. We stopped at last in front of our gate and then he turned to me and said huskily in a comic accent, 'What about that good-night kiss then?' The passionate glinting of his spectacles turned me right off. I got out quickly and said, 'Thanks a lot, Sy. I really enjoyed it.' I went in at the gate and up the path, picked out the key and opened the front door, and he was still sitting there like a lost dog. I waved cheerily at him, shut the door, turned off the light and went upstairs to my room. I don't know how long he waited in the road.

I cleaned off my make-up with lotion and undressed. I knew I'd drop hints about our wonderful evening, but it hadn't been. Mum had remembered to turn on my electric blanket, and I was pleased about that. My party dress was still lying over the chair so I put it back in the cupboard. As I hung it up, I saw that something was bulging the pocket. It was a pair of tights – the black ones I'd worn to Bella's. They looked as if they'd been in a fight. I dropped them into the wastebin, and went to bed.

5

It's after four. The others have left the classroom. They have collected their books, clapped shut the desks one after another, gone home for a last panicky swot.

Their voices still echo in my ears, clattering like pebbles in surf. They make no more sense to me than that.

I am still sitting at my desk. I am pushing down the top with both hands as if there is something inside struggling to get out. My own stacked books await the homeward journey, but I am not thinking about work. I am staring straight ahead at the blackboard, but whether it retains anything of the last lesson, I neither know nor care.

The door opens behind me. A pause, then an elderly tread, stiff, precise, approaches down the aisle between the lines of desks.

'Is that you, Elizabeth?' Silence. 'Are you waiting for someone?'

Now she's close, she can see my face. 'What's the matter, dear? Is something wrong?'

'I'm okay.' What makes me say that? What else can I say?

Miss Soper looks at me. She is kind, she is concerned. She would like to help, I can see. But she is generations out of date. Confide in your mother dear she was young once she loves you you can trust her is the best that she could say.

'You're not ill, are you?'

'No.'

'Is something wrong at home?'

'No!'

'You're not worrying about the papers? Surely you're the last person to have to worry about them!' A reassuring, totally mirthless laugh.

'I'd better go home.' I get up, clasp my books to my chest.

'That's right. Now take my advice, and don't touch any work. Have your tea, make yourself a nice Ovaltine or Horlicks, get an early night. Are you lying awake worrying when you ought to be going to sleep?'

'I suppose so.'

'What do you worry about?' Busily intent on helping, because I haven't yet slapped her down. Her eyes are almost colourless behind her glasses with pinkish frames; I have a sudden, morbid desire to know what she was like in the faraway days of her youth. A dizzy blonde? Brilliantly clever? Most schools would have retired her long ago, with a clock or whatever gift a lifetime of devoted service merits. Here she is a sort of housekeeper, she talks to the man who looks after the central heating, she walks about the canteen at lunchtime, I think she teaches something. Now she is waiting to lock the classroom door. Her question hangs between us and I answer it with a grim joke that will pass right over her innocent head—

'Maths, mostly. Human biology—'

She chips in, triumphantly. '*Maths*, Elizabeth? But Mrs Jacobs is very *pleased* with your maths!' The key snaps shut the lock. We walk side by side down the passage. 'I've heard her mention you by name, more than once, in the staff room. It's never been anything but praise. I'm sure you've no need to worry about *maths*! Now don't forget to put on your coat. You girls! Specially at exam time!'

She even pats me on the shoulder, as I am forced within touching distance by the doorway. She believes she's helped. She actually looks cheerful for once!

Maths!

If *It* came on the twenty-first of November (and I know it did, because I marked it on my date-a-day pad) then it was due on December the nineteenth. That's okay; I remember thinking it would be neatly over by Christmas.

The school yard is empty of cars, even the Head has gone

26

home. I wonder whether Miss Soper is already shut into her watchful flat, from which, under the twitched corner of a curtain, she is seeing me off the premises. I don't turn round. I am crossing the asphalt automatically, the monotonous beat of my footsteps like a metronome, I understand why people hang themselves now and then, there is a state of despair, of utter calamity that consumes the mind, blots out the future. *This can't be* and yet it is, and *there is no way through*.

The crucial point is, *did it come in December?* I can't remember. I go over and over the events between the end of term and Christmas and still I can't be sure. I know that I was tired to death on Christmas Day and I think I thought, this is It coming, but if I thought that, why then it can't have come on the nineteenth, as I am as regular as clockwork. I certainly didn't have it when I went out with Sy. Assuming that it came and passed almost unnoticed in the general Christmas rush (I never have a heavy flow as described on the packets) then it should have been with me again by now on the eighteenth of January. So, where is it?

Human biology – maths, Miss Soper, to boggle your virgin mind — in confirmation of which

next morning

a sudden unexpected sickness catches me on the landing

doubles me up retching ripping myself apart

leaves me collapsed on the top step with tears running down my face

Confide in your mother dear who has already offered comfort and is now anxiously putting on the kettle to make you a strengthening cup of tea she loves you you can trust her

but she believes this is exam nerves, how can I break the spell?

'Stay at home, Pidge, if you're sick. Have a day in bed. I'll ring up now and explain.'

Dad emerging from the bathroom, rumpled in pyjamas, wanting to know what's the matter.

'I'm okay, I'm absolutely okay, stop *fussing!*'

'But you're all upset, it's not like you, can't you tell me what's wrong?'

'There is nothing wrong, Mother, and I am going in, okay?'

Straighten the skirt and tie, soldier downstairs, spike her guns by eating breakfast. Swing off to school as usual, this is Elizabeth as we know her on exam mornings. She'll see Dad off and then have a long chat with her friend Doris, whose spotty daughter is a couple of years younger.

Is Mum really so loving-and-giving, Dad such a monster of ambition? Are Chrissie and Pete genuine super-wets? What about Ann? Does she fill the role of Honourable Best Friend even when she's off duty? I've got into a habit of classifying people, that's the trouble, and now I find myself surrounded by these cardboard types, just when I need a human face.

We sat exams in Hall, which in itself lent solemnity to the occasion. Rows of desks strategically placed to prevent overlooking, lines of royal blue cardigans studiously hunched. The breathlessness of the air disturbed by an occasional cough, a sigh, the rustle of paper. More than once I met the eye of the invigilator, who happened to be, this morning, Miss Soper. It didn't occur to me that I wasn't concentrating. It didn't seem strange to be lost in thoughts that had never before come to me during exams. Bella Rossi, for instance, at the desk on my left – I was fascinated by her writing, large and round, quickly covering sheet after sheet without blot or alteration. A polished performance. Marjorie Parkinson in the far corner already looked as if she wanted to cry. Ann was writing steadily, pausing to think, feeling my gaze and glancing at me with a smile, carrying on writing. So I looked at the question paper and answered the first sheet without effort or inspiration, and wondered what would happen if I was *taken sick* again. Or supposing I suddenly said, I think I'm pregnant, what would happen? Electric shockwave? People ripping up their papers in hysterical excitement? Or would the words fade, suffocated by twenty-nine intellects parroting assorted facts accumulated over the last two precious years? Miss Soper was staring, definitely staring at me. I dealt with another question. I felt extraordinarily bored. What was the point of mocks? The very name was against them.

Ann said at break, 'Not bad. What do you think?'

'Futile. I know I've done badly.'

'You couldn't, not on that paper!'

'I don't care how I do.'

I'd said that before, but she knew at once that this time I meant it, and she looked at me with a surprised, assessing expression. Our conversation then turned to other things.

As we strolled back to Hall for the second half, I said, 'We could go for a walk after school perhaps.'

'I'm afraid I ought to rush home. I've been having nightmares in Latin for weeks!'

Of course if I'd told her the purpose of this walk, she'd have agreed at once. But I didn't.

I thought about Ann a good deal, while all round me people were struggling with equations. I had always hero-worshipped her in a way, from those distant days when she wore a pinafore over her cotton frock, both handmade by her mother, and inspiring me to make little suits for Chrissie's dolls. For even then I admired that sort of house and family. Her background put her at a distance from everyone else. She was friendly, she was popular – but she was different. Sometimes her mother still made her an outfit, not because they were short of money, but because she enjoyed doing it. And they enjoyed living in their higgledy-piggledy house. They were a close unit, you couldn't imagine Mrs Robinson discussing Ann with a friend, as I knew Mum did me. This difference, this closeness, made them strong.

The invigilator, one of the science teachers, was walking on creaky crêpe soles down the lane between the desks. She stopped beside me.

'Is anything the matter, Elizabeth?'

Yes, I think I'm pregnant. This enormous possibility has swamped all sense from these paltry mocks and redirected my thoughts into clear but irrelevant channels. 'No, thank you, Mrs Partridge.' I looked down at my paper and realized that it was blank, without even a name or number.

'You're sure? You look flushed.'

'Yes, thank you.'

She returned to her place. I wrote down answers.

I suspected that Ann was more complete as a person than me. It was all part of the strength. I needed her more than she needed me – one reads that relationships are never equal, teenage magazines are full of this problem. They are also full of my own heart-stopping intellect-bugging dilemma. Could Ann help over that? I mean, would it help me to tell her? What would that do to her opinion of me? No one was more generous than Ann. But now I saw that this Thing, this unimaginable, feared and loathed Circumstance made a barrier – not only between her and me, but between me and every girl in the room, including the few Ann and I bitched over in private, speculating on whether they slept around. (Incidentally they'd be sure to know what to do next, but I certainly wasn't going to ask them.)

After school I walked by myself along the river. There'd been a lot of rain and it was full and swift. Now and then I stopped and stared into it. It wasn't paintbox tints, but the colour of the end of things – greys and browns, and a greenish browny black that hardly seemed a colour at all, but a state of dissolution. I stared at the water until I felt myself leaning, impelled towards it, and then I walked on. As the sky darkened, the river seemed to gain in speed and noise. The twigs I threw in were whirled away.

At last the road dwindled to a path along it, and the houses drew back, as if they'd had enough of such a rowdy neighbour, and left it to tumble and rush through a straggling park. The only amenities were a few plastic litter bins, and a line of more or less broken seats. I climbed on every seat, and jumped down. I ran until I could hardly breathe. This was what girls had done in the past, to try to dislodge a 'trouble'. This was the preliminary to the backstreet abortionist, the knitting needle. I was hot with these thoughts as well as the running and jumping. I was hot with anger that I, Elizabeth, had to behave like an oldtime housemaid.

There was a tiny tots' playground in that park, with metal frames for climbing and spinning. It was surrounded by a rickety paling to keep out older children, but I got in easily. I climbed and spun, hung by my knees, leapt from the highest elevations. It was rage, and hatred too, that drove me on. I could have broken every bone in my body, I wouldn't have cared.

After a while an old man came along with a dog. He was smoking and wearing a cap and the dog was on a lead. They passed quite close to the playground. The man must have seen me but he said nothing. For some reason he brought me to my senses. I stood panting in this little arena fenced out of the depressed park; around, on an incline like a Greek theatre, the terraces of observant houses were marked with orange and yellow lights. I got out presently and started to walk home.

Mum must have been listening for the gate and she had the door open before I could get out my key. She was red in the face.

'Where on earth have you been?'

'I went for a walk.'

'But it's nearly ten! I've been frantic! When I rang the Robinsons and found you weren't there . . .'

Dad loomed in the passage. 'Why didn't you let us know?'

'Sorry sorry sorry. I didn't have any money for the phone.'

'What do you want to eat?' asked Mum as if it was the last straw, pushing past us both into the kitchen.

'Nothing. I'm not hungry. I'm going to bed.'

'I'll bring you up a drink.'

I stopped on the stairs and glared over the banisters. 'I don't want a drink.'

'Don't you talk to your mother like that,' said Dad unexpectedly.

'Leave me alone then, will you?'

His temper flared at once. He said, 'Come down, you! Don't you go slinking off upstairs like that!'

I stayed where I was. I muttered, 'Oh, God – the heavy father bit' – not so that he could hear me.

'What's that? What have you been up to?'

'What do you mean, *up to*? I said, I went for a walk.'

'What about your exams tomorrow?'

'What about them? Last-minute revision doesn't do any good, you ought to know that. I worked all holidays, in case you've forgotten.' Suddenly I started to cry, and couldn't stop. I hate crying, but it was the same sort of impulse as being sick that morning.

Dad looked disconcerted, but he said sneeringly, 'That's right, turn on the water! The easy way out! I'm not pleased with you, Elizabeth. Remember that!' And he went back to his chair, with a hearty slam of the door.

I ran to my room, and slammed my door with such force that several small ornaments fell over. I don't know what Mum was doing during this knockabout. Boiling the kettle probably – she was becoming a compulsive tisane drinker.

And almost at once I had to creep out again, for the box of senna pills in the bathroom cupboard. I took three times the stated dose. Then I got into bed, and lying flat on my back awaited results.

6

Next Saturday I went into London, to a self-service super drug store where there was the least chance of meeting anyone I knew. I walked between the stands in the stark lighting, past wormer pills for pets and winkie neck pillows, horrible plastic bijoux for hair and products to bleach it or remove it, ozone-friendly aids to beauty and diabetic foods. I saw what I wanted on the pharmaceutical counter, but here personal service was provided by a woman in an overall with pepper and salt hair done youthfully in a plait. This was offputting, for I had expected to help myself and pass anonymously by the till. The woman, according to my covert observations as I hovered round bibs and potties, had a slight look of Mum and might offer counselling. It took me more minutes to gather my courage; then I walked forward, took a packet, and handed it to her with my toughest expression. So she kept her suggestions to a sympathetic smile, which I did not return, receiving my wrapped parcel and marching out of the store – and stupidly colliding in the doorway with Mrs Rossi, also going out, small and burly in her fur, who smiled, and surely noticed my state of shock. *Where was she* while I was making my purchase? HAD SHE SEEN? I experienced again the familiar spurt of rage, that I, Elizabeth, had to worry about gossip, even in people I hardly knew or cared about – because things could be suspected – repeated –.

'Up for shopping?' I nodded, grinned. 'No work books? Like Bella, she's gone out with friends. You do your best, that's what I tell her, that's all you can do. Good luck, dear.'

She went my way, I pretended to be going the other, and regained my bus stop by a circular route.

The house was empty when I got back, but still I locked myself in the bathroom. Then I opened the packet. At first it was surprisingly difficult to understand the instructions. My face got hot and I avoided my eyes in the mirror above the basin. But after all I wasn't a fool, and this home diagnostic kit had been designed by experts to be as simple as possible. The illustrations were clear enough. There was half a page of questions and answers for those morons who even then had failed to make sense of the test. And there were two tests included in the packet.

Ten minutes later, the first little scoop showed unmistakeably pink. I stared at it with a thumping heart.

What was the point of doing it again? Five minutes later, I was doubly sure.

I gathered the bits and pushed them into the chemist's bag, rolled that in a newspaper, went outside and shoved it well down in the bin under a heap of rubbish. Just in time – Mum was back. I wiped my hands quickly on the grass but hadn't time to get indoors. She looked at me in surprise through the kitchen window.

'Hi! Isn't it a lovely day!' I hadn't noticed. She joined me in the garden. 'It's just so incredibly warm. I said to Doris, it's a positive pleasure standing on street corners on a day like this. I hardly needed my jacket.'

'How did you get on?' Retarded baby day. Perhaps my baby would be retarded. She'd be able to take it with her and people would buy more flags. I hated I hated my baby. I realized that I was pinching my fingers together with impotent rage. But Mum was crouching over the daffodils which were already poking up in clumps through the grass.

'All right. It's a popular cause. Most people give something. Not like Lifeboats. Do look, Pidge, there's buds already! Maybe they'll flower on my birthday.' That was in February. Mine was in August. I'd have to bring it forward a few months, when I went to the Family Planning.

We went inside and she turned at once to the kettle. I said

34

nastily, 'You ought to cut out the tea. You're becoming an addict.'

'That's not fair. I haven't had a cup all day!' I looked at her, and no doubt because I was upset, the cardboard mother suddenly slipped and I had a glimpse of her real face. Well, it was crazy not to talk to her! *She was just so nice.* But there was my pride in the way. I didn't want her compassion, I didn't want her solutions. This was my problem and I was going to sort it out myself. Besides, how would she keep it from Dad?

'What's the matter, Pidge?' she suddenly, quietly asked – woman to woman, as you might say.

'Nothing!' The lightness of my tone!

A pregnant (ha!) pause.

'I tell you what,' she said in a different voice. 'No tea. We'll open a bottle of Pomagne. How about that? We'll celebrate!'

'*Celebrate!* What are we celebrating?'

'The end of your mocks? Nearly the end of them, anyway. Anything you like! The daffodils in the garden!'

'Your birthday next month.'

'Nice!' She scrabbled happily in the drawer for the corkscrew. But I'd have got rid of my Problem by then. That's what I was thinking.

7

I said I was Jenny Davis, sixteen last August; I said that I lived at Number 13, Butterfield Rise (13 for obvious reasons, Butterfield because there were several in that area). I said that my doctor's name was Lazarus – I hadn't been expecting that question, and I called him that because I had just done a divinity paper. I gave his address as the practice Ann went to.

'Quite a long way from your home, isn't he?' mused the clinic doctor.

I agreed, but I said he was a family friend, and that was why I couldn't go to him now for advice. She accepted this, and didn't query anything else. She asked for the date of my last period, and then she said, 'Slip off your jeans and panties, and pop up on the couch, and we'll have a little look.'

I felt my face burn. I said, 'You don't need to, I did two tests, I know I'm pregnant.'

'I'm afraid I must examine you myself, or there's no question of taking this any further. It's easy to make a mistake, and if you aren't pregnant, all your troubles will be over!' She added, 'There's really no need to feel embarrassed. You'd be surprised how many girls I see, and you all look very alike!'

She was kind, she was careful, in no way did she make me feel I'd done anything stupid or wrong. When it was over I felt totally cast down. I couldn't look her in the face. I can't remember anything about her except her voice, which was pleasant.

We sat facing each other with her desk between us, and I stared at the curtains. She confirmed that I was pregnant, and wanted to know whether I'd considered telling my mother.

'No.'

This she thought was the first thing I should do. Mums, she said, usually hit the roof, but when they came down again they were surprisingly helpful and understanding, more often than not. She advised me at some length to confide in her. What about Dad?

'He'd kill me.'

Immediate concern in the voice. Did I mean that I feared actual physical violence from my father? I saw the lever and grabbed it. 'Yes.'

'Has he been violent with you in the past?'

He'd never struck either of us, Chrissie or me, but there was always that twinge of a suspicion in the back of my mind that he might. I think that, oddly enough, I the favourite feared him more than she did.

'He's just that sort of person. He's always been like it.'

'But with your mother helping—'

'It wouldn't make any difference.'

She leant back in her chair and I knew she was looking at me, thought I was now staring at the filing cabinet. 'Oh dear,' she said. 'You are in a bit of a mess.'

Then the consulting room was quiet until her watch suddenly bleeped for the hour and broke the spell.

'And you're perfectly certain you want to terminate your pregnancy?'

'I am perfectly certain.' My tone of voice surprised both of us. She probably linked it with Dad.

'There's not a shadow of a doubt in your mind?'

'No.' I felt like a swimmer who's almost made it to the shore, the golden beach where there are happy, normal people. But no – she poured in more water.

'All right. Now I'm going to make you another appointment, for tomorrow – you can come again tomorrow? I want you to see one of my colleagues, she's very young, not much older than you, and the two of you can talk it all through so that you're quite sure you're making the right decision.'

'I don't want to talk to anyone else,' I said. 'I've already made the decision.'

'Yes, dear, you're very determined, but even though you've left things rather late you mustn't be allowed to rush into this. You see for instance she could be there with you when you break it to your mother, if that's what you decide to do; this is all part of her training. Believe me I wouldn't suggest it if I wasn't anxious for you, if I wasn't sure you'd find it a help.'

I went away feeling I'd been thumping at a punch ball stuffed with foam.

Luckily we'd just finished mocks so Mum and Dad weren't surprised that I wanted to be out late two nights running. I made the journey back to the clinic with my feelings of despair and apprehension – for after all the biggest hurdle was yet to come – heavily overlaid with rage. All this emotion must be indelibly lining my face, by the time I was twenty I'd look an old woman! But I just loathed being pulled about by all these people in the name of welfare. I didn't need their help, I didn't want their nosey advice. I knew what I wanted, which was the most sensible thing for me in my circumstances.

The social worker had her own little office with posters of pop stars on the walls and a coffee machine. She gave me a plastic container of grey coffee and we settled down on beanbags to talk. Everything looked grubby but that may have been the light which came from a bleak bar in the ceiling. She had spots and long thin chestnut hair, she wore face powder and loose mauve and purple clothes. She said, 'Two Jennies!' with a silly laugh, and I looked blank, until she explained that she was called Jenny too. Then I couldn't remember what surname I'd given, or the number of my house, and I turned hot with panic. But she didn't ask about any of that. She looked at me with her round brown eyes the size of stewed prunes, and she said, 'You know there's no need to feel embarrassed.'

'I'm not.'

She smiled knowingly and went on about getting me sorted out and how it was worse really for girls who came from what she called privileged homes because their families tended to be very shocked when they made this sort of mistake. But I wasn't to worry about it because that was the sort of home she came from herself so she knew what I was up against. She could only say that she was absolutely on my side, she'd do everything she could and there was a lot she could do. All this was only the beginning of the spiel, she liked talking and she was used to a captive audience. I judged from her expression which was both holy and smug that she enjoyed her power, and it made me sick to look at her. So I stared at a picture of Prince and after a while she noticed it and broke off and said, 'He's gorgeous, isn't he?'

'Is he?'

Her expression sharpened but she said very sweetly, after an awkward pause, 'More coffee?'

'No, thanks. I'm wasting your time,' I said. 'I'm not going to discuss this with my parents and I want an abortion. Nothing you say will make me change my mind.'

'I'm not trying to do that. I just want you to be aware of all the possibilities. It's my responsibility, and I wouldn't dream of calling it a waste of time. I'm glad to do it, really I am, it's the least I can do.'

So I had to put up with it.

At last the lady doctor looked in and Jenny said brightly that we had had a thorough in-depth discussion and she was sure that I understood all the aspects of my situation, and the help that she could offer. Then they both looked at me, and I said, 'Will you fix for me to have this baby taken away please?' I was still very angry but I was also very tired, and I sounded desperate. The doctor went away to make a telephone call, and Jenny talked about post-termination counselling. I hoped she would spend a long time finding Butterfield Rise, and, if it existed, even longer searching for me in it. But I did leave that clinic with a hospital appointment in my pocket.

I had to see Mr Barrett at St Floy's at four o'clock next Wednesday, and stay in overnight. He would do the operation the following morning, and all being well, I would be able to leave the hospital in the afternoon. Overnight! That was a complication. How was I going to clear that with Mum and Dad?

All the way home I racked my brains, trying to think of an alibi, while the familiar impotent fury kept distracting me. It was totally unreasonable of them to expect me, at fifteen, to account for all my movements. There were girls in my class (not Ann, not Bella) who were allowed to come and go as they pleased; nobody at their homes dared to check up on them – I'd heard them boast about it. It was stupid of Mum, as well as unreasonable, because obviously I'd leave home as soon as I could and that would be that. The middle-aged woman across the gangway kept looking at me, until I felt like putting my tongue out. Then I realized that the vehemence of my thoughts was making my lips twitch, and a warm wet drop on the back of my hand turned out to be a tear unconsciously shed. Oh, God! Now she was directing a tentative smile at me. I slammed into a different seat (the bus wasn't crowded) out of her view.

Chrissie? I never stayed there, and Mum wouldn't fall for that, she'd be on the phone to her immediately. Ann? It had to be, because there was nobody else. I would have to tell all to the person I loved and respected most in the world, and what would she think of me then? (Another tear, or two.) She'd help, I could count on that, but things would be different between us. Our relationship would be marred. This is me, Elizabeth, I am clever, good-looking, successful, and I have just one friend I can turn to. What has gone wrong with my life?

Next day I broached the subject as we were walking back from games together. She couldn't know how my heart was thumping as I said, casually, 'I've got to be away from home one night next week. Can I tell Mum I'm with you?'

A hair's breadth of a pause. Then she said, 'I should think so.' She wasn't going to probe. Her tone was too carefully noncommittal; that was unbearable. I blurted out, 'I've got to go to hospital. I don't want her to know.'

She stopped dead and stared at me in horror. 'Oh, Pidge! I've been wondering what was the matter with you. You're not ill, are you?'

You see the real reason just didn't occur to her. What way was there of telling her the truth? I stammered, 'It's the overnight bit that makes it so tricky, and next day – Can you say I'm absent with a migraine?'

'But why are they keeping you in?'

'Oh – tests or something – '

'*Tests?* What on?'

'Blood. Heart I suppose.'

'You mean they think you might – '

'Just in case. There won't be anything wrong.'

'But your Mum – I know I'd want mine along.'

'It's different for you.'

She thought about that. She said, 'You mean you've set all this up on your own? I think you're incredibly brave, Pidge.'

I didn't answer. I wanted to cry. I hadn't meant my confession to turn out like this with a big cheer for Elizabeth. It was the first time I had deceived her, and in a way, it was like saying goodbye. Girls passed us in twos and threes, wearing shorts and carrying hockey sticks. The sun was already going down behind a row of poplars that marked the far end of the park. I'd often noticed the effect without thinking about it in words, but this afternoon the stripped trees looked like captive flames, cones of red and gold.

Within the deepening blue overhead, some birds were flying slowly to wherever they sheltered at night. What was this choking feeling of things coming to an end?

We reached the school entrance, dumped our games kit into the lockers and buttoned on our skirts, collected our prep. Ann and I always made a pair and there was chance after chance to say, 'Look, you've got it wrong. I'm not being brave, I'm pregnant. I'm not saving Mum agony. The fact is, I daren't tell her.' But I couldn't. The trouble was that whenever we'd talked about It happening to Us, we'd always decided to Keep the Baby. We'd always judged it a mean, selfish act to dispose of another living being utterly dependent on us, for reasons of convenience. This we felt was the Right decision, and in our ideas we were very aware of what was right, and always heroic.

Ann was meeting her mother for tea out and evening shopping. She invited me along but I refused. At the gate she asked, out of the blue, 'How soon will you know?'

'Right away, I should think.'

'That's something, at any rate.' She gave me a cheering smile and ran to the car where her mother was waiting. I walked home. Wednesday lay ahead of me in a blur of fright. But afterwards – in fact, in one week from today – I'd be beginning to forget the whole thing. Wouldn't I?

8

Our family doesn't go in for believing in God. Starting with Gran: if you're discussing religion, her little wrinkled face will sharpen, and as soon as she can butt in she'll tell you that what she can't get over is the way religious people behave when they aren't in church. According to her they spend the week fiddling their tax returns, committing adultery, abusing their children or knocking down old people on pedestrian crossings, and she always winds up with the exclamation, 'And he calls himself a *church*goer!' (north-country accent charged with righteous outrage).

Dad refuses to talk about anything remotely metaphysical. He starts shuffling his feet irritably and rustling the paper, and if pressed gets up and leaves the room. As for Mum, she'll tell you brightly that she doesn't know about *God*, but she does believe in *People*. (Remember that with typical illogicality, they fixed for Chrissie to marry Pete in church with me as bridesmaid, before sending them on honeymoon to what Gran calls the Bally Arricks.)

Even so it's tempting to suspect that there is an Eye watching, a Finger moving the pieces on the board. Because something happened to me that night in the hospital that is bound to affect my whole life; and it's comforting to think that somehow, somewhere, it fits into a Design.

I have to admit that it was a predictable encounter. They put me in the gynae ward because both single rooms were full, and that was horrible, any spirit I had left, quickly drained away. I was the youngest there. Most were middle-aged ladies in frilled nylon nighties, pushing their fluffy slippers along as though they were tired out. They didn't

43

seem to remember that their clothes were pretty well transparent, which shocked me. I imagined they'd all had hysterectomies, and that they guessed what I was in for. I felt an outcast. I'd forgotten to bring a book so I went into the day room and got some papers, sat down on the side of my bed and pretended to read. The screens and trolleys made a grim rattle. Perhaps Chrissie would be here in twenty years, her time of youth and beauty wasted, dragging herself around as if she'd spent her life sleep-walking.

Thank God poor childless Chrissie had no idea what I was doing at this moment. Where would they throw my bit of a baby? Would it go with the waste and end up in the smoke which puffed at intervals from the tall hospital chimney, a landmark for miles around? I hadn't talked to Mr Barrett, who had discussed me with Sister as if I wasn't in the room. Our eyes had met just once, and I knew immediately that he had daughters of his own, and didn't much like what he was looking at.

We all went to bed, but there was no sleeping in the half-light, among the pale blankets and flimsy curtains, with dread of tomorrow like strangling hands round my throat. After a while I slid out and went to the loo. I opened the door and I was inside before there was time to realize what was happening. A woman by the basins was crying as if her heart would break. Her forehead was pressed against the glass for coolness, and as soon as I entered she saw me in the mirror. She was a lot older than me – mid-thirties at least – while I looked, as I could see all too well, even younger than I am, no more than a child, standing by the door scarlet with embarrassment with my mouth open. She wiped at her hair and tried to smile, which was worse than her tears. She said, 'Sorry, dear, do you want to come in here? You carry on, don't take any notice of me.'

'I'll find another one.'

'That's all right, I don't mind, it's nice to have a bit of company.'

So I used the toilet, perching so that she wasn't disturbed by any vulgar noise. When I came out, she'd washed her face and arranged herself, but she still looked awful. She needed to talk to someone and I was that person. I turned on the taps and kept my eyes on my fingers and the swirling water.

'There's worse things happen every day, don't you worry! We're lucky in lots of ways - well, we've been married twelve years and never a cross word, that has to be a record! It's twelve years of waiting and hoping, that's the trouble, and now this.'

I couldn't shut out the monologue. I didn't look, but I could tell from her voice that she'd started crying again. Lady Macbeth, Pontius Pilate – I washed and washed.

'We shouldn't have given him a name. It makes them into a person. Dad – I call him Dad – he said, right at the beginning when I told him, 'You know how I feel? Chuffed!' So that's what we called him, in private like. Our Chuffey. The one thing we wanted, and it's been taken from us!'

Stick to reality, this is shades of Gran, pure sentiment, emotion. No angel of destiny could look like this blotched, miscarried mother with her damp hair and washbag with a jumbo pattern. And escape – escape as quickly as possible.

'It's waking in the night, that's the cruel thing. When the pills have worn off, and the disappointment comes flooding back. Oh, Chuffey!'

In her distress it couldn't matter any more whether I was listening. Along the corridor there was a lighted office for the night staff; I looked timidly in and reported her. Then I went back to the ward and got into bed. I lay on my back and spread my hands over my belly where secretly, invisibly, this other person was feeding and forming. He had been thrust by the meanest kind of opportunist and thief into my body, which had no means of rejecting him. And still I would go on nourishing him, against all inclination and judgement, until that last second when he was sucked away.

Just as I was going to sleep I was aware of the Chuffey

woman moving up the ward in the dimness, gently guided by Sister to her bed at the end. Then all was still, but she stayed in my dream. She was with Mum and Chrissie, the three of them sitting on a bridge with their bare feet dangling almost to the water. Mum's hairstyles are always significant and this was loose, covering her shoulders with youthful chestnut waves. They were all very much present, in a way that felt more actual than a dream, and they were talking animatedly together, but I couldn't hear what they said; I suppose I was somewhere on the bank because their voices were drowned by the noise of the river. At last a paddle boat came along, clattering and banging, with a loudspeaker that quacked, 'Wakey wakey girls!' It was the early morning tea trolley in fact, and time to surface.

I got out of bed feeling well and clear-headed and resolved. I removed my nightcase from the locker, went to the toilets and locked myself in. Then I washed and dressed and did my hair, stuffed my overnight gear into the case and walked out. My knees and hands were trembling but I was perfectly sure in my mind and ready to defy anyone who tried to stop me. An elderly man was mopping out the entrance hall, and he opened one of the glass doors for me. It was cold and grey and drizzling with rain, but there was a bus stop conveniently close, and I took the next bus without looking at the number, and put several miles between me and St Floy's before getting off for refreshments.

Don't ask me what my plans were for the future. For the present I made a pig of myself, devouring two helpings of egg and chips, a bun and two large-sized milks. (Eating for two. MILK BUILDS BONES.) I was in a euphoric state. It was as if I'd stumbled on to a conveyor belt going in a particular direction where basically I didn't want to go, and at the last minute I'd pulled myself together and jumped off. When I'd finished my meal I found the local library and settled down in the children's department. I read some Just Williams which I hadn't looked at for years, and giggled over them without any inhibitions as that corner, on a school day, was deserted. Hours passed without a single serious or constructive thought crossing my mind; giddy relief was all I felt. And then it was time to travel homewards. First stop was the sandwich bar near school, where Ann and I were regular customers. The girl behind the counter was nice, and generous with facilities. I had left my uniform there overnight; now I changed back into it, and walked home.

I did experience some chilling of the courage as I went up the path. How was I going to tell Mum and Dad? What was I going to do if I didn't? But that could be left to the future. All along, you may note, I'd tried to put off taking decisions until circumstances pushed me into them. That isn't like me, and it isn't a good idea either.

Mum heard me on the stairs and looked out of the kitchen. 'Hi! Had a good time?'

What were Ann and I meant to have been doing? 'Yes, thanks.' Something in my tone encouraged her because she came out, smiling and friendly. She never bears a grudge, and now she seemed to have forgotten that I'd been snapping at her for weeks. 'You've got a letter, it's in your room. Don't be long, your tea's ready,' and she returned, humming, to the stove.

The writing on the envelope looked young, but I didn't recognize it. I opened it. It was a get-well-soon card from Steve, Ann's brother. Underneath she had written, 'I swear I haven't told anybody else. All our love, A.'

I tore it into small small pieces. Nice of them, but if Mum found it it would upset the applecart so to speak.

During the course of the evening she remarked, 'You look better than you have for weeks. It's those wretched exams! They ought to be done away with.'

Dad jerked his leg irritably. 'What a damfool thing to say! How else are you going to separate the sheep from the goats?'

'I thought the changes were meant to make it less stressful. It's worse than ever, as far as I can see.'

'A bit of stress never hurt anyone. Anyway, our Pidge thrives on it.'

Ding dong, they argued it out. Dad was so sure that I was a sheep. I wouldn't be able to lie over my results – our school encourages parent involvement, and Mum and Dad never missed a meeting. Worry worry worry – there was a big row coming.

9

The Mocks Bomb burst over Sunday lunch. Chrissie and Pete were with us as usual, and Mum had just doled out seconds of nut cutlets and salad at her end of the table, while Dad and I stuffed pork and greens. Fletcher the dog had his head on my knee; he was soppy but no fool, and he knew which meat-eater was likely to slip him fat and gristle. Dad suddenly raised his head and looked at me, and said, 'Let's have your results then!'

I should have been prepared for this. I should have remembered that he often played golf on Sunday mornings with the parents of someone in my class. She wasn't very bright, and it is a nasty human attribute to feel that success is more so when somebody else doesn't have it. So his face was already set in lines of pleasurable anticipation, and when his eyes met mine the two bright spots in them seemed to say, You and I, Pidge, are zooming to the top. I could see the black pinpoints of his beard although he always shaved very tight, the skin where it was perpetually struggling to get out was paler than the rest of his face, as if the razor removed a layer. All this I knew by heart from my usual seat opposite him, but saw like new in the seconds before I answered his question, plus a blob of gravy on his chin that glistened because it was a dark day and we had the light on. And I saw something else: a flicker of doubt across his face; but it vanished instantly because he believed that with me, doubt was not possible.

Here goes! 'Do you really want to know? They're bloody awful as a matter of fact.' Making this brash statement I was conscious of sudden chill round the knees. The canny dog had removed himself to fawn on Pete.

Then I had to watch Dad's face deepen to the colour of mulberries, the sparks in his eyes switch off. I didn't speak, but inside I was shouting, What did *you* ever achieve, you git? Why take it out of me, you ignorant sod? Obscenities to stiffen my back, harden my mouth and eyes – because he was dangerous all right, and deep down I knew it, deep down I was afraid. But that he mustn't see. I could quell him with arrogance.

I turned to Mum and said, 'Please can I have some salad?'

'Of course.' She held out her hand for my plate as if nothing was happening. Chrissie's face was a study of shut shutters. Pete had turned pale with fear, and it made me want to thump him.

Dad growled, 'I don't like your language.'

'Sorry sorry!' I ate lettuce in composed forkfuls.

'I'd like an explanation of what you just said.'

'Perhaps we could talk about it another time,' suggested Mum.

'Shut up!' he snarled, rounding on her.

That should have been enough to cow the tender-hearted mother, but instead she drew herself up and her eyes flashed. It suddenly struck me that Dad's furious outbursts, which had cast such a shadow over Chrissie's life, and mine, were not entirely offensive to her. She was a natural actress, and 'Young Mother Defies Savage Oppression' was one of her meatiest parts.

She said severely, 'Pidge was off-colour when she sat those exams. I should have thought even you would have noticed it.'

He said to me, 'Do you mean you failed the lot?'

I pretended to consider. Then I said lightly, 'Not quite all. I think I had a C in maths.'

'A C in maths,' he repeated. His voice was hardly human.

Chrissie got up and started to clear the table. I suppose she couldn't bear to sit there any more, but it was a mistake – I could have told her. Dad suddenly picked up his plate and slammed it down on to the floor. The remains of his meal shot about, I got potato on the ankle. There was a shocked silence among the sane members of the family, punctuated by his breathing, and Fletcher clearing the bits surreptitiously.

Quite suddenly I started to laugh. Four pairs of eyes instantly turned on me. They must have thought I'd flipped. So I tried to put their minds at rest. I gobbled and gulped, 'It really is funny. They're rubbish exams.' But I saw at once from Dad's face that I was only making it worse; indeed now they were all looking fussed, even Pete knew how I felt about my work. But, please, what are mocks, compared with what I've got up my sleeve, or rather, down my front? Maybe now would be a good time to spill the beans, when Dad couldn't have much rage left in him. Instead I made an effort to pull myself together, and said more calmly, 'I've done all the work. I'll be okay in the summer.'

Then Fletcher began to howl because he had cut his mouth. Chrissie and Pete hauled him into the kitchen for first aid, and I followed and began to stack the dishwasher. None of us wanted any pudding. Soon I left the house to meet Ann at the sports club we belonged to. Mum and Dad were still sitting at the table. Maybe they spent all afternoon chewing over my prospects; I didn't care. Ann and I slammed away on the squash court and I went back with her to tea. Afterwards we continued the Monopoly game we'd started last weekend, with her parents and Steve playing. So it was a quick good night and straight to bed when at last I got home.

Chance after chance to talk to Ann – and I didn't. I'd told her my tests were all okay and dropped the subject, knowing that she was the last person to bring it up again. It did alter the basis of our relationship a little. Before, she had the parents, the home, the lifestyle I admired (not envied, but I did admire it), but now I had my secret (leukaemia scare? brain tumour? women's problems?) that I was being brave about, and she respected my silence. So naturally I found it increasingly awkward to tell her that I was pregnant. What a letdown!

I just felt exceedingly well during those remaining weeks of the spring term. I ate a lot, I played hockey so hard that people muttered about aggression. After that one bout of sickness, I had no more trouble, and I simply dropped the baby from my mind. The development of the foetus was laid out in our biology books, but I never looked at it. It didn't show, even in sports gear. I'd always been cautious in the gym, good enough but careful. Now I hurled myself at the horse and the box, dangled from the ceiling on the ropes, swung by my knees. But the baby clung like a limpet. And I must start making plans. I wanted to be able to say to Mum, 'Look, this has happened, and this is what I'm going to do about it.' That was the way I'd always run my life, with Mum on the receiving end. But now I seemed to have a mental block. I couldn't think of anything beyond the enjoyment of these weeks at school, and that was lucky, because they were my last, as it turned out.

One afternoon I phoned Mum from school to tell her that I'd be late back – she insisted on this, as if the roads between us were barbed with kidnappers and rapists. For once we didn't have our usual conversation, 'It's me, I'll be home late, around nine, can you keep supper, okay? 'Bye,' slam, click. This time for the first time she said, 'Oh no – *not* late – *please* not! Is it important? This is something special.'

What could be special? She'd had her birthday; Dad's wasn't for ages. 'What's special about tonight?' I sounded grudging, suspicious.

'I'm not telling, it's a surprise.' And she hung up.

Surprise? I slouched home, swinging my bag, feeling thoroughly grumpy; let myself in, dumped my books in the hall, chucked my coat over the banisters. 'In here!' she called from the kitchen.

I went in. We used to keep a few vases of dried flowers round the house, and she had picked out some of the brighter blooms and braided them into her hair. The plaits had fuzzed out, so that the effect was strange, particularly as she was wearing jeans and an anorak. Then my gaze dropped to the table and I saw that it was covered with holiday brochures, this year's Mediterranean glamour for you to choose from in the privacy of your home. My God! What had she been up to?

'I've booked for Greece,' she said. 'Two weeks!' She was still out of breath with excitement.

'Great!' I said. 'When are you going?'

There fell a sudden silence.

'Us. The three of us.' No comment possible from me. 'I've rung Dad at the office. I think he's pleased.'

Total washout of spirits, plummeting of the heart. To hide my face I turned to the fridge and made a business of getting out the milk, and rummaged in the cupboard for a glass. I said, 'But you don't want me along.'

She sat down suddenly. It was as if she'd been bounding from a trampoline – higher and higher on imagined pleasures and delights – and I had abruptly pulled it away and she had come thumping down to terra firma. That's the trouble with Mum. She will rise to these planes. She said, 'You mean you don't want to come.'

'I didn't say that! I just thought it might be nice for you and Dad. Like a second honeymoon.'

'But you're the whole reason for doing it!'

'*I* am! What d'you mean?'

'I've been thinking that you, and Dad too for that matter, could do with a break. It's not much of a holiday for any of us if all we do is visit Uncle Jerry –' true, true – 'and I suddenly thought, before you're completely grown-up and spend all your time away from us (which is how it ought to be and don't think I mind because I don't), it would be nice to go away together. So today I Took My Ring.' She didn't need to specify which – she only had one, bar her engagement and wedding rings. It had belonged to her mother, and past

53

financial crises had been lit by this possibility: I can always Take My Ring. And now she had done it, spent the value on two weeks in the sun for the three of us.

'That's great,' I said again. It didn't sound specially convincing. I looked round for the biscuits.

'You *are* pleased? You've been saying for years—'

Yes, Ann and I had had a project. In our year off, we were going to Greece. We were going to Delphi, Corinth, Olympia, Mycenae, working as chambermaids or waitresses when our money ran out, moving on from island to island. Every now and then one of us, usually Ann, would add a magical, factual detail, as, 'We'll take the night ferry to Thassos because you can smell the pine trees before you see the island,' or, 'We might be able to work on the new archaeological site on Santorini.'

'When are we going?'

'Soon! The first two weeks in April. It's only a package – the last one they had available. So I snapped it up. I just thought it would be so perfect, getting away from everything into the sun, just the three of us. (No, I don't feel mean about Chrissie. She'll be so pleased for us, and after all we did give them their honeymoon.) Dad couldn't believe it. When he comes to he'll be thrilled to bits, and of course it's always been top of your list, Pidge.'

From what unguarded chat had she divined how much Greece meant to me? It had always been my number one fantasy country – my *Shangri-la*, as the Head would say. One shouldn't speak, one shouldn't even think at home. They prise everything out.

'Lucky old you,' said Ann when I told her next day. It didn't seem to strike her as a disaster. 'Think of me as you stride up the Acropolis.'

'It isn't Athens, it's Crete. Some scruffy holiday resort on the north coast between Hania and Heraklion. I wish I wasn't going.'

'Knossos, Phaestos, Gortyna. Make the most of it. Think

54

of me dragging my feet in the dear old suburb. I think you're incredibly lucky.'

'Don't you see how they'll wreck it?'

'But we're going back.'

'I won't want to.'

10

Odysseus waded ashore. His eyes were black, deepset, he had black wavy hair and a moustache; he wore a white shirt open to the waist and grey trousers rolled above the knee. I had been watching him for some time, beachcombing as I thought. Now he came towards me, carrying a plastic bag, his bare feet flexing to the rough shape of the rocks. When he was close he stooped, and selecting one from his catch, cleaned it with a scooping movement of his glittering pocket knife. Then he bent towards me, offering a sea urchin.

I took it. He made a charade of how to eat it, but I hesitated, suspecting it might have a symbolic significance, it might mean I was bound to kiss him; afraid too, I must confess, that it was polluted – Dad was appalled by the sewage disposal set-up. But the fisherman guessed what was in my mind and he was already cleaning a second, drinking from the shell to demonstrate how delicious, how harmless. Now it seemed churlish to refuse. The spiky shell was like a horse chestnut. What it contained tasted of peaches that had grown in the sea.

'You like?'

'Wonderful!'

He prepared several more. I had to consume them, under his brooding gaze.

'You German?'

'No. I'm British.'

He pulled an identity card out of his pocket. The picture had been taken some years ago. I couldn't read his name. I noticed that he was thirty-nine.

'You lonely?'

'Me? No! Not at all. My parents are just round the corner.'
I wished they would appear. With the cliff behind me, and
rocks on each side, a quick getaway was impossible. Besides,
he wasn't being nasty. He was behaving in a perfectly
natural, friendly way. I didn't want to overreact, I didn't
want to hurt his feelings.

'You like swim?'

'Not today, thanks.' My heart beating fast. I guessed that
if I'd been Greek, he wouldn't have been interested; but
then, if I'd been Greek, perhaps I wouldn't have been sitting
here alone. He was drawn by the callow tourist. And then I
caught sight of Mum and Dad, swimming in strongly with
their snorkels. I waved, and gave them a shout.

'Tomorrow,' he said. He didn't seem at all offended. He
strolled away over the rocks with his bag of urchins,
muscular, unhurried.

Dad called from a distance, 'Come in and join us! The
water's really warm today.'

'I left my suit at the hotel!'

'Run back and get it then. Or swim in your pants, there's
nobody to see.'

'I'm okay. I like paddling.'

'Stop making excuses! You're missing half the fun of the
holiday!'

And they kept telling me how marvellous it was, so that in
the end I couldn't resist it. I kept my top on. It would soon
dry in the sun and wind.

Around three we had our picnic, fruit and cheese, on the
beach. The wet cotton clung to my body. Dad looked
sideways at me and said, 'Our Pidge is putting on weight!'

My face went red. Mum said quickly, 'Don't make
personal remarks! I know I'm grateful for my elastic-waisted
skirt. I must have put on a kilo.' After lunch she sat in the
shade and wrote postcards. She really enjoyed fitting her
enthusiasms into that little space, but I didn't and I didn't
write any; I had already bought Ann a leather wallet which

smelt of goat. I lay at a distance digesting my meal, with my dry skirt heaped over me disguisingly, and it was then, when I felt so relaxed, so light that I was almost dissolving into air, that my baby gave a twist and a jump.

So strange! So familiar! I knew him at once – not, repeat not to be confused with the digestive process. I covered him with my hands and waited breathlessly for the next sign of life, which happened almost at once, barely moving the surface, but vigorous inside.

'What's the joke?' Dad's voice.

I opened my eyes. His smiling face darkly excluded most of the sky.

I said, 'I must have been dreaming.'

Dreaming, yes – a nightmare, with my heart thumping in my throat! If he knew, wouldn't he rip me open, wrench out and crush the child? Before the smile faded from his face! All in the bloodiest Greek myth tradition!

There was a taverna in the old harbour where we usually went for supper. I would have gone to different places, but Mum and Dad liked the feeling of belonging, being recognized, having certain specialities recommended because the waiter had had time to gauge their tastes. The tables were set out on the jetty under an awning, with checked cloths secured against the wind. Ours – always the same – was nose to nose with a boat which never seemed to leave her moorings, though others slipped in or out, dropping orange light across the oily water. Mum and Dad now had the habit of holding hands after the meal, and taking a long time over their coffee and raki. Sometimes I left them to it and walked back to the hotel alone; sometimes I waited, observing them and the animated scene.

Mum had made a superlative effort over her appearance for this trip, and thanks to an expensive lotion, her fair skin had turned a beautiful golden brown. Even her zany hairstyles didn't seem out of place here. Dad had tanned almost as dark as a Greek, and his silver hair looked actorish and bold. His body, what with the golf and now swimming, looked good in brief cotton clothes. I'd been afraid that he'd get on the wrong side of the Greeks and their way of life, call them twisters or layabouts, but he was just relaxing more and more; indeed both my parents were very cheerful and amorous. They laughed at me for ignoring the continual passes any girl gets in Greece, and made jokes about 'thawing out our frozen Pidge'. I played up to it to amuse them; in fact the three of us were getting on as well as Mum could possibly have hoped. But sooner or later it had to come to an end, the happiness, and the holiday. The days were flicking past.

On the last morning, Dad made a drama of buying a present for Mum. He didn't want me along, so we went for a walk together. Then again my heartbeat quickened with apprehension, for this would be the best possible time to Tell All. Over the fortnight we'd reached a better understanding than we'd ever had; for I had always assumed that she loved Chrissie best, since Dad so obviously preferred me. But recently it had dawned on me that that was not necessarily so. We were actually arm in arm, dodging the crazy traffic that zipped down the narrow streets, slowing each other to peer into the leather shops, the greengrocers where boxes of bright fruit stood well out into the road, the touristy shops where tiny pinafores and embroidered woolly coats swung on little hangers in the wind. Chance, chance! Embroidered baby shoes leading to purchase and confession! I dithered about, touching things, while the proprietress watched me with a smile that was kind but impersonal, as if what amused her was much beyond me – an eccentricity in nature, or even God. Then Mum said, 'I know, Pidge. If only Chrissie . . . ', in a tone of sympathy and sadness, as if she'd guessed what I was thinking about. And that of course completely blew it. I left the shop without buying anything. We walked away without speaking, and our linked arms no longer made a bond; I hated her now for jumping to conclusions, and I didn't want to touch her any more.

Dad had said he would meet us at our usual beach, which was beyond the town, out of range he hoped of the sewage outflow. Anyone who has been there will remember the road which runs along the sea, skirting the Venetian fortress that once defended Rethymnon. From it the view opens across the bay towards Hania, with huge mountains on the left that at this time of year were thickly covered in snow. It had all been so much more beautiful, so much more pleasant than I had expected; but now as I padded along with Mum, I felt that this was the end of the happy days. I had had a respite, which was now over; the worry of the baby struck me again, worse than ever; I felt now that it was too much to bear. Dear old Mum thought I was sad because we were leaving. She said, 'We'll come back, next year maybe, it'll be something to save for.'

We were going to have lunch out, as well as supper, because it was our last day. We had discovered that the lady in the square white house not far from the beach, who sold drinks, would, if asked, produce lamb cutlets and chips, or an omelette. So when Dad turned up, we sat at a table in her little garden, which was across the road from the house. I call it a garden but it was only a few olive trees, surrounded by a low, whitewashed wall. The omelettes were made with very yellow eggs, but they tasted nice. Dad had the cutlets, very brown and crunchy, but plenty of them. They drank retsina, I had a coke. We had just finished when Mum started to cry. She does this sometimes; it is her emotional contribution to an occasion, for instance a birthday, or Chrissie's wedding when she wept happily all through the service. So the rest of the family isn't necessarily concerned, but Dad put his arm round her, and she sobbed, 'It's just I wish Mum was here to see how happy her ring has made us.'

'It was money well spent, my love,' he told her, and that was certainly true for them. But I couldn't help adding logically, 'If she was here, you wouldn't have had it to spend.'

This struck a jarring note. Dad gave me some money and asked me to settle the bill.

The square white house was dark inside. I waited by the counter for several minutes before the woman came out with a piece of paper and totted up what we owed. She had large, clear greeny-blue eyes and again, the smile – the oddly impersonal smile that I had noticed here. It was not cosy, it was not ingratiating. It gave nothing away. No matter how often we sat at the table under the old olive trees, that smile would never alter. It would remain detached. It belonged to a different culture.

She spoke no English at all, but she must have guessed that we were leaving tomorrow. She accompanied me to the doorway of the big room which was more like a garage with its concrete floor and no downstairs windows. We stood side by side staring across the road, through the garden to the sea which was blue, and the sky which was blue and blue to whatever depth skies reach. I was sad right up to my throat, I could have cried out with pain. I needed to say goodbye quickly and go; Mum and Dad had already left the garden and were strolling hand in hand up the road. She glanced at them, and then suddenly all the beaming radiance of her eyes fell on my face. It wasn't wisdom or knowledge or sympathy or understanding. I can only describe it as light. She raised her hand and just touched my cheek, before returning inside. That touch was a talisman of some sort. Her eyes were the kind that are painted on the prows of boats, for fishermen to find the way.

Mum and Dad were purposely loitering and it would have been easy to catch them up. Instead I picked my way outside the garden wall in the direction of the beach. There was part of an ancient fountain in that wall, a carved animal head with a broken spout. The old olive trees, and the wide amounts of blue in air and water, made it feel like a holy place. Zeus might have descended on it in one of his fanciful disguises. It might have been that woman – long, long ago – that he came for.

One last swim. I looked carefully round; the rocky shore, the sea were deserted, indeed the only other person I'd seen here was Odysseus, and he never appeared before four. I stripped off to my pants and slipped into the water. I'd had to be so careful with my loose-fitting tops, pretending I was worried about sunburn, and this was heavenly, like slough-ing a skin, like casting off chains. Soon I was far out where the little waves were dancing. Why not swim on, swim until the sea took me away and solved everything? But I turned and flogged in, of course, before it was too late.

The beach felt hard, alien after so long in the water. I lay down out of the wind, dog tired, with hardly the strength left to move a finger. For some reason I started to think about Ann. I decided to tell her everything as soon as we met, no more prevaricating. Now even the idea of talking to her was a relief. I imagined how the conversation would go, I visual-ized the scene so completely that if I'd heard her voice I wouldn't have been surprised.

But it was Mum's voice I heard. She said, 'Elizabeth.' My proper name, said in such a tone – it was a surprise and a shock. I jerked awake, snatched for my clothes, sat up and looked round. She had come up behind me over the rocks. Heaven knows how long she had been there. It was immediately obvious that she had seen – everything.

'*What have you been up to?*' she said in a hoarse, odd voice.

That was too much, that question. It belonged to the days when I'd gone off on my bike without telling her, or nicked a bit of housekeeping money for sweets. It was insulting in this context. What did she think I was? If she'd started with 'Love –' how different things might have been!

I didn't answer, or look at her again. I was pulling on my clothes. In the distance I noticed Odysseus poking about in shallow water. After four, it must be – I'd lost all sense of time, which was a pity.

'Elizabeth, you and I have got to talk,' said Mum. No rubbish now about taking my arm – indeed a quick glance confirmed that any contact was likely to be violent. Old bag and hypocrite, when she spent so much time flogging flags for the underprivileged who, after all, come in all shapes and sizes! Her face was chalk-white under the enhancing suntan. She then said the worst thing, in my opinion, that it was possible for her to say. She asked, 'Is this Sy?'

I was speechless with astonishment, and immediately after, fury. Was that what she thought of my friends? Gran's comments flicked across my mind. 'You cow!' I said.

She slapped my face. I swore. 'If you do that again I'll thump you!'

We stared at each other over our heaving bosoms. She had struck me exactly on the spot where I had felt the touch of the Greek lady. When I realized this it made me want to cry. But Mum was remembering, too late, the articles she'd studied with Doris about being understanding and not having rows with your teenagers, and she was making visible efforts to control herself. How I loathed her! We'd lived together for nearly sixteen years – wasn't I more real than the woman's page problems?

Odysseus was moving closer. 'Come on,' snapped Mum. She led the way back to the road. Neither of us spoke. Never let me return to that beach, or to that sea, or to the fountain where the holy water has dried in the spout, under the twisted olives. The magic is broken, the peace, the beauty shattered.

The road at this time of day was lethal with vehicles of all sorts, loaded with oranges and hurtling to the town. Dad in particular had been amused by this, by the wild driving which would have maddened him in our country, by the crazy contrivances for hauling fruit. But Mum and I trudged along in grim silence. I didn't expect her to speak before we reached the privacy of the hotel bedroom, but when we turned off into the quieter suburb, she altered her pace to walk beside me, and said, 'I'd just like to know how you're going to break it to your father.'

'Don't you tell him! I'll never forgive you if you do.'

'I hardly think you're in a position to threaten me, Elizabeth.' There was no answer to such an idiotic statement. She seemed to think she'd scored, and went on more confidently, 'You mean you had no intention of telling him. Or me.'

'You aren't very easy to talk to.'

'What more do you want!'

Silence again as we walked up a quiet street. There were rugs and counterpanes hung out over the balconies to air. Someone was watering window boxes. Someone was practising with a clarinet, the same phrase again and again. Oh never let me return to that flowering street, for it is burning up around me, it is ashes under my feet!

Dad was waiting near the hotel. I said I was going to pack, and Mum said she'd help. I was about to snap back, but we were bound to have a showdown and it might as well be now. I didn't dread it any more. I felt tired – tired to the core. Dad told us that he would go and look for a gorgeous Greek girl, and he went away, grinning, while we got the lift to my room. Inside she went to my bed and sat down, and then she said, 'This was the holiday of my lifetime, and you have wrecked it.' She was not acting, she was simply stating a fact. She then said, 'How far on is it?' The clinic doctor had used a warmer tone.

I told her. I had my back to her, emptying the chest of drawers into my bag. 'Oh, my God –' she was starting, hysterically, but I cut her short. I told her how it had happened. Then there was a silence.

'But people do get tight at parties,' she said.

'I know.'

My window looked straight out to sea. There was a fishing

64

boat, broadside on, chugging in to the old harbour. People were bathing from the hotel beach, but it wasn't crowded; we'd been told that thousands more would arrive by the end of the month. The seaside bars and cafés were being painted in readiness.

'But Pidge, for heaven's sake, why didn't you tell me at once? It would have been so easy then to do something about it. Something like this, that really isn't your fault. . . . Even if you couldn't say, you should have gone straight to the doctor.'

'I did.' I told her about the clinic then, and St Floy's. As I finished she sat staring at me as if I was completely mad.

'You mean you went in to have it done, and *walked out*? *Why*?'

'I couldn't go through with it.'

'But having got yourself to that point. . . . Have you any idea how serious this is?'

'Of course! I'm not a fool.'

She looked at me as if she doubted that. She said, 'Well, at least I know now. I'll consult Bobby as soon as we get back.' She meant our family doctor. 'What did you think you were going to do, anyway? Were you going to mention it at all?'

'Yes, I suppose so. Anyway I shall go away in the summer.'

'What do you mean, *go away*? To have the baby, do you mean?'

'What else?' I muttered. It did sound pretty silly, in words.

'So the baby will pop out, like shelling peas, and you'll leave it on somebody's doorstep, and swan home as if nothing had happened? Is that what you mean?'

'There's no difficulty finding homes for babies. There's queues of couples wanting to adopt.'

Then Chrissie and Pete came into my mind, and probably into hers as well. Neither of us spoke for several minutes. I spotted Dad. He was standing near the large soil pipe, thinly covered with sand, that marked the boundary of the hotel beach. She said, more harshly than before, 'You can put any idea of having this baby out of your mind. The only thing you can be sure of about the father is that he's a bad lot. As for you, it would mean disaster – do you hear that? Don't look at me like that, Elizabeth! You'd better listen to me for once! You're in a mess – all right, I'm not blaming you, but it's happened, and it's got to be stopped. Be your age! Can't you see, your whole future's at stake! You have to take these exams in the summer.'

'Why shouldn't I? The baby won't stop me.'

'You are really naive!' she exclaimed, emphasizing those four words. 'You don't seem to understand *at all* what being pregnant involves – in spite of failing most of your mocks! I thought biology was your star subject! You don't seem to know anything!'

She glanced at her watch and got off the bed. 'I'll have to go and get ready for supper. Have you finished packing?'

'Yes.'

Dad was moving slowly up the beach. He caught sight of us in the window and smiled and waved. Mum said soberly. 'How we're going to tell him I just don't know. He's got such an opinion of you. It'll break his heart.'

That was meant to stab mine. I detest sentimental blackmail. I said coldly, 'I expect he'll get over it.'

She looked at me with dislike. 'You're a tough little bit, aren't you?' She said bit, not bitch.

'I'll do the telling, anyway.'

'You're welcome! Have the decency to leave it until we get home, that's all.'

'Don't worry!'

I'd forgotten the presents.

Mum got a dessert service, blue porcelain with a white bird design. Mine was soft, in crumpled tissue paper that had been used before. It was a blue sun dress with a full skirt and elasticated top, and ribbons that tied on the shoulders –

very simple, something I'd seen in a shop window and wanted at once but couldn't afford. If he'd looked for a fortnight he couldn't have found anything nicer. If he'd wanted to cover me with shame, he couldn't have hit on a better way.

'Dad! You shouldn't have! All your money!'

'That's all right,' he said, grinning, embarrassed. 'Let's see you wear it, that's all!' It made him angry when he gave me clothes and I never put them on. But this was perfect. 'Go on!' he said. 'You've got ten minutes to change.'

I glanced desperately at Mum, but she said nothing. She didn't care if I spent our last evening in coals of fire.

Later, when we were alone for a few minutes, I said, 'I've been thinking it over and I've decided I don't want him to know. I don't mind anything but that.' It sounded heroic, on a par with Deciding to Keep the Baby.

Mum said, 'What on earth do you mean? You haven't any choice!' She paused to let this sink in, then continued, 'Your attitude to Dad and me is really strange. You don't seem to see us as separate people. We're like accessories to yourself, when you think about us at all. It's as if you're so obsessed with yourself, you haven't got time for anybody else.' She paused again before adding the final blow. 'Chrissie isn't even an accessory!'

I was hot all through at the injustice of this, but I didn't mean to be deflected. I repeated urgently, 'There's no reason he should know. Dr Kennedy will sort it out if you talk to him. I can go into hospital and we can call it wisdom teeth or something.'

'Wisdom is the last thing you've got!' snapped Mum. She looked pale and too old for the scented flower she had fastened in her hair. 'For hospital read private clinic, and ask yourself who'll have to foot the bill. You're a monster of egotism! You don't seem to love us at all. Don't you understand anything? Okay, fair enough to keep it quiet if it could have been done at once. But this is a lot more serious. I shall tell him if you won't.' Her voice died away, her expression changed to false jollity, and I realized that Dad was coming up behind me, before I felt his hand on my bare shoulder. He sat down between us and looked at me; it was a long, straight look, but he didn't ask any questions. Instead he insisted on buying me a Mount Parnassus, which was a particularly lavish ice cream, and he and Mum sat over coffee until I had finished it.

11

Chrissie had laid a cold supper for us, and switched on the heating, and arranged a bunch of flowers on the kitchen windowsill.She had done her best for the Homecoming, only she had overlooked the fact that Fletcher had made a mess on the garden path. Dad trod in it, and walked upstairs with the suitcases before anyone noticed. This put him in a bad temper, which made home immediately all too familiar.

Next morning he was off to the golf club to dazzle them with his suntan and Greek island stories, before I came down to breakfast. When I had finished I got my bike out of the shed, and went after him. It was much colder than Crete, but it was still a lovely morning, windy and sunny, and the gardens were bright with flowers. I felt optimistic as I pedalled along, imagining the conversation. (In my experience this is always a mistake, and a waste of time.) The best thing was to come straight to the point. Listen, Dad, I guess you realized while we were on holiday that there was something important I have to talk to you about. The trouble is I've kept putting it off because of not wanting to upset you. . . . Then he would be anxious to know what it was, and he would probably protest that he wouldn't be upset. So I would go on, The fact is I do hate it when you're cross and any father would be furious about this but truthfully it isn't my fault, I couldn't help it. . . . I realized my lips were moving and I pressed them tightly together. I went on with the fantasy. I would tell him about Bella's party and too much to drink, and the rest of it. Then he would be absolutely enraged and want to kill the boy responsible. But I didn't see, I honestly didn't see why I should get bollocked too much.

I had reached the club by this time. I glanced into the bar and it was empty, so I went out on to the course. Soon I saw him in the distance, with a man I didn't know. I followed and kept clear until they had finished the game, and then we went back to the clubhouse together. This gave me a different view – which is always disconcerting – of the irascible parent who ruled our home.

His companion was grey-haired, tall and heavy, with an air of authority. He remarked politely, 'Your daughter, Kenneth?' I was surprised – everyone calls Dad Ken.

'Yes. This is Elizabeth.'

He smiled at me. 'Do you play golf?'

I would have answered, but Dad chipped in. 'Tennis, squash, badminton, those are her games. Between ourselves she's pretty good, but she hasn't time to do more. GCSEs in the summer.'

'Bad luck! I expect they cast a bit of a shadow.'

I managed to say, 'They do a bit,' before my father replied, 'Elizabeth likes exams. She works hard and she gets the results. She's one of the lucky ones.'

Glancing at me, his companion must have read my expression, for he said kindly, 'It's an asset, you know; so many clever people are put off by a printed paper.'

'She doesn't mind,' said Dad. 'She's ambitious. She wants to be a vet.'

'A vet!' repeated the grey-haired man. He sounded impressed. 'You must be pretty bright.'

'She is,' said Dad. We walked on for a while in silence.

'Did you have a good time in Crete?' I guessed the tall man had been cudgelling his brains for a topic.

'Yes, thanks.'

'Two weeks of sun and sea,' said Dad carelessly, spinning and catching a golf ball, speaking as if it was something we could do whenever we liked. 'Very relaxing.'

'What did you think of Knossos?' he asked me.

'We didn't go there.'

'Really? Oh, you should have had a look. People either rave about it, or else – or else they don't, you know,' he ended lamely.

'She didn't want to drag her uneducated parents round the sites,' said Dad. As this was the truth, it was mortifying to hear him say it, without the slightest resentment.

'It wasn't that sort of holiday.'

Dad said, 'People have been asking me what we did, and I don't know what to say. The fact is, we just enjoyed being together. We're lucky that way. It strikes me,' he said sagely, as if he'd done a lot of thinking before coming to this totally trite concolusion, 'when people complain to me about their teenage kids, I sometimes wonder whether it isn't they themselves, the parents, that are to blame!'

'Could be,' said the tall man. 'Could well be. And now I think I see my wife waiting for me in the car park – no, thanks, she's a tee-totaller, and I'm afraid I'm already late back. Goodbye, Elizabeth, and good luck to you!' He walked rapidly away. All the parked cars looked empty to me. But perhaps he was telling the truth.

Dad took my arm and gave it a squeeze. 'Now that man, Pidge, is a bone surgeon, and a very successful one. He can charge God knows what for a consultation. That's what I like about golf, you meet all sorts. All sorts,' he repeated, scanning the groups in the now crowded bar, pushing the door with his free hand. 'Come on, I'll introduce you to more of my friends. We must do this more often.'

'No, thanks, Dad, I've got the bike. I want to go back now.'

'Sure? Sure you don't want a coke or anything?'

'No, thanks.'

'Tell Mum to expect me soonest.' He whisked inside. I cycled home. My mood had changed to one of black despair. Until now I'd rather enjoyed my pedestal, gone along with the part of Ken's clever daughter. Now I saw that when I fell, he would be crushed.

Mum was in the kitchen when I got back, wearing the Cretan apron I'd given her which was probably made somewhere else (I hadn't checked). She was tossing a salad. She saw at once from my face that I hadn't spoken. 'I didn't have a chance,' I said.

Today Chrissie and Pete were invited to supper, which seemed more ceremonial for the presentation of the table-cloth and napkins we had brought them. Dad was very late for lunch. As I had the bike out, I rode over to Ann's in the afternoon, but she was away, so that was a wasted journey.

Some boys were kicking a football in the park. Perhaps one of them was my baby's father. Perhaps this mean-looking man in a mac, archetype of flasher or child abuser – perhaps he'd got into Bella's under cover of darkness and thrust his foul sperm into me. It made me sick. I sped past him through a puddle, spraying his legs with muddy water. Perhaps he – or he –. There was no way of knowing. I never would know.

Next morning Mum said, 'Bobby's away until tomorrow. I've made an appointment for both of us.'

'But I go back to school tomorrow!'

'You'll have to take the day off. We're seeing Dr Kennedy at eleven. What about Dad?'

'What about him? *He*'s not coming with us, for God's sake!'

'You know what I mean. Have you spoken to him?'

'I said, there wasn't a chance.' Mum thinned her lips as if that was typical prevarication on my part. I went on loudly, 'I couldn't get him alone at the club. Chrissie and Pete were here all evening. What do you expect?'

'You to pull yourself together and grow up. You seem to have lost all sense of reality. You seem to think that if you don't do anything, it'll go away!'

This made me very angry. I shouted, 'It's difficult, don't you understand? It's bloody difficult for me!'

She said coldly, 'If you have to swear, please keep your voice down. I don't want the whole street to hear.'

I slammed out of the house, got the bike, rode round to the Robinsons'. Ann heard the gate and looked out of her bedroom window.

'Hi! I thought it was today you flew in from foreign parts. When did you get back? Hang on, I'll come down and let you in.'

Her parents were out; Steve was already back at school. I followed her into the kitchen.

'Staying for lunch?'

'Okay – thanks.'

She got out the sliced bread and plugged in the sandwich toaster. 'Go on – was it brilliant?'

'Some of it. It was more okay than I thought it would be.'

'Did you do any of the Things?'

'No way! I kept all that for when we go.'

No sense of reality! How could I go back? Mum's words, *This was the holiday of my life and you have wrecked it*. I thought I'd buried that lot but it bobbed up now.

Ann said, 'What's wrong, Pidge?'

'It was all wrong at the end.'

Then this gap, this chasm opened again between us. It should have been possible to bring out the well-rehearsed spiel, I'm pregnant you see, and Mum found out. So she's pressuring me to tell Dad and get rid of the baby. I dare not tell him – look, it's not myself I'm thinking about, but him. I'm scared *for him*. Anyway, I've got to persuade our doctor to help me make a deal with Mum. Okay, I'll ditch the baby but *Dad mustn't know*. There's no reason why he should. We can call it anything – wisdom teeth is the most likely, that's all – why can't she see that it would be *better for him*?

Ann said, sounding alarmed, 'Pidge, what's the matter?'

I felt tears running down my nose. I am Elizabeth her friend who never cries. When she saw that I was not capable of replying, she went through to the sitting room, where the drinks were kept, and I heard her opening the cupboard. She came back with the end of a bottle of sherry, and emptied it into a glass for me. She said, 'It isn't your fault. You and your parents are just incompatible – totally and utterly incompatible.'

'I know,' I sobbed. 'It's a pity. It seems crazy to have spent all those years together and not to be able to discuss anything or even understand what hurts another person, or ever make allowances or try to see a different point of view.'

'It can be difficult.' Ann had her back to me. She was trying to fit the sandwiches into the toaster but they were too bulky for the compartments.

'But you can talk to yours,' I said.

'I suppose so. If I got pregnant I don't quite know how I'd put it across. Or drugs –'

My heart had started to thump. I blew my nose and said, speaking through the tissue, 'Your parents are really understanding. You could tell them anything – even about drugs I should think, or a baby. They'd know how to help.'

'Yes, but it's the initial shattering of the image that would be so awful. You know how they think of you as a special sort of person . . . . This is bloody awful, this toaster.'

'We can eat them raw.'

'No, the bread and the cheese are rigid with staleness, from before the weekend . . . . I don't know how you'd get round that one.'

'You would have to tell them?'

'Yes, of course.'

'Even your father?'

'Specially my father.'

'Why specially him?'

'I don't know, but it's true. I suppose fathers feel specially about daughters, so that lands us with a *certain responsibility*, as Soapy would say.'

'But then he'd never forgive you.' Damn tears. Thank God she was still chopping away at the sandwiches.

'Of course he would!'

'Mine wouldn't.'

She switched on the toaster. 'He would, you know. I've noticed his face at times. He really believes you're the greatest.'

'I wish he didn't, that's all! It's hell to live up to.'

'You're doing okay.'

There was a sudden smell of burning cheese, and she turned to the sandwiches. She is the soul of tact and I'm not, but I am more perceptive. I would have spotted my problem immediately.

I stayed there until Steve got back from school, and then I biked home. Our house was empty, and the calendar revealed that they had gone to supper with Doris. So I made certain preparations, and went to bed early. I lay and thought everything over carefully, and again, carefully; I didn't want to rush into more mistakes. I had my bank book and some clothes; I remembered towels and got out of bed, took two and added them to my bag. I had all my school books, my Walkman and favourite tapes.

This was my time for making a plan, working out with scientific precision what action to take tomorrow. The stupid thing was that my brain refused to tackle it. It kept going off at a tangent – visualizing the parental reaction, for instance, or inventing the 'Farewell Letter – a complete waste of time because I'd already decided that there was nothing more to say. You're so right, Mum – it's the same idea that if I don't sort out my problems, they'll go away. A childish feeling that somebody else will do it for me, and I'll wake up and find it's all over.

Dear Mum, I'm going because you've failed me – that's all there is to it. This pregnancy isn't my fault, it was a hideous accident, and most of all I needed sympathy, but how quickly you ran out of that! That's very odd because usually you overflow with it, all the unknown deprived and dis-advantaged can count on you. But of course you're such an intense person, you have all these feelings and emotions, you overreact, you always have. And somewhere you feel that I've let you down.

The sad thing is that I've never asked you for anything before – not anything important. I'm sure if anybody had put my case to you in theory, you'd have been confident that you'd know what to do and how to be. But in practice, it's too much. Even the most superficial aspect of it, that it would be so lovely if only it was Chrissie – that shows clearly in your face.

So I'm leaving because I have no alternative. I ought to say, and this is the truth, that I don't blame you. I don't blame myself either. We are totally and utterly incompatible, and there is no way I can go through this crisis at home. N.B. I don't understand, not at all, how you can contemplate doing away with my baby, which by now has a face, and fingers and toes? And go on calling yourself a *caring person*?

I sign my name in my mind. My face, as I do this, is thoughtful but not angry.

Nothing to Dad. Not so much as a P.S.

They usually made an evening of it *chez* Doris, and I wasn't expecting them back before midnight. But then it suddenly occurred to me, what if Mum, who might be having slight pangs of guilt after this morning's tiff, looked in to see if I was all right? She'd get a bit of a shock at the sight of two packed bags, drawers pulled out, wardrobe standing open and the dressing table cleared. So I nipped down and wrote, 'Safe home and in bed, good night' on a bit of kitchen paper and left it on the little table in the hall where they couldn't fail to see it; and I hung the ceramic swot notice PLEASE DO NOT DISTURB on its nail on my door. Then I locked myself in and went back to bed and turned the light off.

Within ten minutes I heard the car returning. This was a nasty surprise, for it was not yet eleven. What had happened? I was lying as usual on my back with my hands spread over my stomach. My eyes were wide open in the dark, I seemed to be listening all over. Presently they came in by the kitchen, and I heard Dad on the stairs, I knew at once from the sounds that he was furious. Immediately I started to shake. My God! Mum had told him. She hadn't been able to resist the drama (with Doris as chorus – after all you've done for her Ken one tries to be understanding but it is just too bad). Oh Mum, I shan't ever forgive you for this, *he'll burst in*, and now here he comes shouting in his horrible other-voice, 'No, I'm going to see her and have it out, you can't stop me, the two-faced little slag!' – over to Mum holding the reins with typical heroism, 'No, Ken, no, let her sleep, you can have it out in the morning. You won't get any sense out of her now.' So the battle raged to and fro, and certainly would have woken me if I had been asleep. Finally they crashed off to bed. I guessed they had had several drinks. I didn't stop shaking for a long time.

Dad had a habit of going to the loo in the middle of the night, around one or two. I had to wait for that. Then, when the house was again quiet, I dressed quickly, and opened my bedroom window. He had only yesterday unscrewed and removed the home-made double glazing, which made things much easier for me. My window gave on to the roof of the kitchen extension, and from there it was an easy drop on to grass which was soft and squashy at this time of year. I let the bags go first. Then I checked on my bank book and card once more, thrust the Walkman into my jacket pocket, and jumped down. No problem! as they say in Greece. This is me, Elizabeth, in the act of leaving home, which I always expected to do as soon as possible, but hadn't visualized before in quite this way.

How to fill in the hours before daylight and transport, that was the question. I hustled up the narrow path between the fenced back gardens, and came out into a parallel, quiet street. Almost at once I saw the lights and heard the drone of an approaching car, and shrank back into the shadows. Just in time: it was a police panda, moving from A to B in the nightly fight against crime perhaps, but looking more as if it was cruising around, passing the time. No reason to think it would come back this way, and soon I emerged and went on up the street. The bag of school books in particular seemed to weigh ten times as much as usual, but even so I was glad to have them. I didn't mean to spend the next five months doing nothing.

After a while my frenetic energy ran out, and I sat down on a wall and wondered where I was going. I could have sheltered in Ann's garage, or probably their car – the Robinsons never locked anything. But I didn't want to involve them even inadvertently, and besides I knew that that was where Mum and Dad would start looking for me. So although I passed the garden, and the dark and silent house where I had spent the most cheerful parts of my life, I didn't go in. Ahead lay the arterial road with its orange lights; their glare showed in the distance, and I could hear the roar of traffic even at this hour. Beyond lay a cheaper sprawl of development, where Chrissie and Pete were buying their first home.

As soon as I remembered that, I made up my mind. I picked up my bags and set off again, aiming to cross the main road at an inconspicuous point in case any nosey cops turned up and asked what I was doing. I scuttled across in a lull in the traffic, and was soon lost among the prefabricated brick boxes with their tiny fenced gardens. Literally, lost – because although I knew that Chrissie lived in Wildoak Lane, I couldn't remember the number. Why should I? I'd never wanted to go there before. So I trudged down this very long road, and suddenly I remembered that they lived opposite a health food shop, she had said how handy it was. So back I trailed, and crossed the road, and peered in at the huge front window. There hung the orange lampshade I'd given them for Christmas!

I didn't intend to knock on the door. I wasn't planning to spoil Mum's big chance in the Pregnant Daughter Walks

Out episode. However, I had forgotten Fletcher. He was stretched out asleep on the sofa under the big window, and just as I noticed him, the telepathic pet opened his eyes and instantly sprang to life. Attempts to reveal to him who I was were futile, he began barking hysterically, and soon lights were flicking on all over the place. Through the open plan I saw Pete hurrying to unlock the front door, and presently he appeared in the porch in his M & S towelling bathrobe, and there I was totally at a loss, pale as a ghost no doubt, with a crammed bag in each hand. His bluish feet were bare and I noticed that his toenails were clean but needed cutting. He said in a whisper cracking with astonishment, '*Liz*! What are you doing here?'

There seemed no point in beating about the bush so I answered, 'I've left home.'

Folk were stirring angrily in the adjacent houses and Pete looked round uneasily. He said, 'Well, you'd better come in,' and stood back, and I pushed past him. We went into the front room. He quelled Fletcher and turned off the lights, explaining, 'We mustn't wake Chrissie. She's only just gone to sleep.' He looked at my bags. 'Are you thinking of moving in here?'

'No way!'

He looked relieved. 'What's happened?'

'I'm pregnant.'

Then there was silence. Fletcher was muttering and licking himself, the clock ticked, somebody was belting home on a motorbike. But the silence between the two of us was absolute.

I said, 'It was an accident, I got drunk. That makes it worse in a way. Disgusting, isn't it?'

'I don't know what to say.'

'Don't bother. I didn't mean to get you up. I was going to spend the night in your shed, that's all. I'd have been gone by morning, but stupid old Fletcher—'

'He's a great watchdog.' He rubbed the old bonehead

affectionately. I noted his embarrassment; as for me, all inhibitions had flown. The unreal light helped, the outer glare filtered through Chrissie's fisherman's net curtains. It was like sharing confidences when you stay the night with a friend. Pete said, 'Do you want any milk or anything?'

'I'd love some.'

He went away. I sat down by Fletcher. My brain was still alert but physically I was exhausted. It was too much, the thought of dragging myself any further.

The milk was hot and nice. He stood watching while I drank it. 'Are you going to tell Chrissie?' he asked.

'No.'

'Where are you going?'

'I can't tell you that. If you don't know, they can't get it out of you. I can't stay at home.'

'But you're coming back.'

'Why should I?'

'But you're – I don't know.'

He seemed to be having a brainstorm over this. I'd never given him any credit for wit, but it did strike me that now, in twilight, without specs, he was really rather good-looking.

'I've got to try to persuade you to change your mind,' he said when he had finished flogging himself, metaphorically speaking.

'How can you do that?'

A hopeless silence.

'You can sleep the night in here if you want. The sofa's big enough for you and Fletcher. He hasn't got fleas,' he added; I was sure of that; Chrissie was paranoid about vermin.

'That's nice of you, Pete.' I meant it. Considering how he feared Dad and adored Mum, it was, very nice.

'The shed would have been useless anyhow. I keep it locked.' He put out his hand for the mug. 'I'll get rid of this. I'll wake you when I come down first thing. You're sure you don't want to see her?'

'Quite sure.'

'Okay.'

'Thanks a lot, Pete.'

He was going away when he had a thought. 'What about money?'

'I've got some.'

'You'd better let me know where you are. I won't pass it on. Somebody's got to know what's happening to you.'

'I can't! Apart from anything else, it wouldn't be fair to you.'

'I can take it. I mean it. Think it over.'

He went back to the kitchen, and I heard him washing the mug, creeping upstairs to my sister. I settled down with Fletcher, who took with natural greed the best part of the sofa, leaving me with one cushion and what should have been a sleepless night. But my baby, which had been perfectly quiet since that day on the beach in Crete, suddenly started moving again, much more strongly now, in a comforting series of loops and springs. He seemed to be telling me that I had made the right decision. So instead of making a plan, even such a basic one as whether to turn right or left at Chrissie's gate, I dropped into a deep and even happy sleep with my face against Fletcher's warm shoulder.

12

Pete brought me some tea at six forty-five, and I was out of the house by seven, having found out the quickest way to the tube, which was such an obvious question that I didn't feel I was giving anything away. I wanted to get out of London, and the town I thought I would make for was Bath. I had been there once on a school trip and liked it. It was large enough to lose myself in, and there was no reason why Mum and Dad should follow me there. I would be living on the breadline, even with the job I had to get, but I had a feeling that I wouldn't sink so low in Bath as I might in the poor parts of London. It seemed an elegant place.

Coach would have been cheaper, but the train was more anonymous. I got off the tube at Paddington. By now they'd have missed me, and they'd have rung Ann and discovered I wasn't there. So Dad would undoubtedly have alerted the police, and among the places they were sure to watch would be the mainline stations. I had meant to use my bank card first, but now I decided to leave as soon as possible. I had about twenty pounds on me, which was the last of my Greek spending money changed back into sterling. I found the ticket office and kept with the crowd. I felt my bags made me conspicuous, but here most people were carrying luggage of some sort.

'Single to Bath, please.' I'd nearly said 'half', bit it back just in time. Fifteen and under is half on British Rail, but people had queried it before because I look older than I am. Now I didn't want anything like that. I didn't want to draw attention to myself in any way.

I was standing in the wrong queue, the official in the next

booth was giving out tickets without any questions. But mine stared at me over the top of his spectacles and asked, 'No Student Railcard?'

'No.'

'But you're a student, yes?'

'Yes – sorry! No.'

The person behind me tried to interrupt. The official raised one hand and said severely, 'One moment, please! Here we all got a train to catch!' To me he said, 'Nineteen pounds fifty please.'

My God! Panic heat rose from my neck to my face as I scrabbled in my wallet. I had the money, with forty-five pence over. The man stamped out my ticket and said, as he passed it through to me, 'Student Railcard don't cost so much and save you one-third on your fares. Pick up a leaflet.'

I joined the crowd staring at the announcements board, feeling flustered. The next train to Bath left in three minutes, but most people were already on it, only a few still hurried through the platform entrance, where there was a soberly dressed woman who seemed to be waiting for someone. She looked to me like a plain-clothes cop. I decided to hang on for the next train and go in with a crowd. I bought some chocolate with the last of my money, and wished I'd asked Pete for a sandwich.

I left the station and asked a newspaper seller the way to the nearest branch of my bank. I walked down the street, trying to blend with the crowd. At every step I expected a tap on the shoulder, a voice to say, 'Aren't you Elizabeth Russell? Follow me please to the Missing Persons Bureau.' Every passing bus, every cab I expected to contain a squad of nimble detectives. When I reached the cashpoint I withdrew my weekly ration of thirty pounds, which left me with less than fifty in my account for emergencies. It would be safest, if I had to make any more withdrawals, to go to Bristol or Chippenham, both towns within easy reach of Bath. I returned to the station with ten minutes to spare. This time I was lucky – a crowd of people about my age, bizarrely dressed, were going on that train, so I simply added myself to the throng. Several even carried bags identical to mine. The lurking woman, if she was a snoop, couldn't be blamed for not spotting me – even though I felt as if MISSING PERSON was daubed all over me.

Once on board, I distanced myself from the hippy types, sat down in a no-smoking corner seat, and stared out of the window. Soon the train began to move, and the journey passed uneventfully. Maybe I should have been having profound thoughts, including a few pangs for the many undoubtedly being suffered by Mum and Dad. But I didn't think about home. I was very tired, and that made me anxious. I didn't know how I was going to manage on my limited funds. Even so, I decided to go bed and breakfast tonight, and tomorrow look for a room and a job. Then I shut my eyes and slept for a bit. I woke to a dreary landscape that seemed to be getting wetter with every mile, while rain dashed against the windows of the speeding train. They'd be filing in for lunch at school. Ann would be worried – she'd have heard from Mum for certain, but she wouldn't have told anyone, she'd still be pretending that I was ill. She'd hurry home after school and ring Mum in case there was any news. And there wouldn't be. And in a week she'd have joined Bella's table, and eventually they'd visit each other for tea and go shopping together, and perhaps Steve would get a crush on Bella. She wasn't much use at sport but she was nice, she was the one either of us would have picked for a friend if we hadn't had each other.

The train stopped at Bath Spa, and I got out. The hippies were getting out here as well, and I followed them through the barrier. The girl beside me said, 'Hi! Why don't you join us?' She had a floppy black felt hat and orange hair that looked as if she never brushed it, a knitted two-piece, black stockings and lace-up shoes. I said, 'No, thanks,' It sounded rather abrupt, and I added, 'I'm meeting someone.' She stared at me with hard blue eyes and said aggressively, 'I don't believe you. You're leaving home. I know the signs.' Several of her friends turned and stared at me then, weirdos with woolly caps and tattered clothes. So that my heart started to knock nervously, but I smiled and said, 'Thanks, anyway,' and I walked away. But the orange-haired girl started to shriek with shrill laughter, and I realized that I was making for a NO EXIT. I swerved off into the ladies, and stayed there until the coast was clear.

I trudged miserably towards the town centre, and as soon as I found a Macdonalds I took refuge inside. The beautiful city I remembered bore no resemblance to this grim, dark place thronged with mackintoshes and umbrellas. I took a long time over my coke and hamburger. But after an hour the sky began to clear and the sun broke through, gleaming on the wet stone and making the puddles shine, and I walked back to a house I had noticed with a B & B sign in the window. It was in a terrace of tall, narrow houses with long, neat, stony gardens, and as I walked up to the door, I had the feeling that I was being peered at from behind the dowdy curtains. Even so I had to wait for several minutes on the top step before a woman answered the bell.

'Excuse me – have you a room for the night?'

'Is it for yourself?' suspiciously.

'Yes please.'

'Just the one, single room?'

'Yes.'

'Just for the one night?'

'Yes.'

A pursing of the lips, as though I was asking a lot. But she let me in, and I followed her up three flights of narrow stairs where a smell of boiling cauliflower lingered, past painted numbered doors, all chipped, all shut. The only room she could offer, apparently, was at the very top of the house. She stood back to let me view the glory of it. It was small, drab and dirty.

'How much is it, please?'

'Fifteen pounds for the one night.'

'Oh.' It seemed a lot. 'Does that include breakfast?'

Reluctantly she inclined her head, adding, 'Bath extra.'

There was a washbasin in the corner, I could make do with that. She said, 'You won't find anything cheaper. Do you want it, or not?'

'Yes please.'

She handed me the key and we went downstairs. I had left my bags in the hall. She said, 'You can pay me now if you like,' and she stood there, so I did. Pocketing the notes, she told me, 'The room's let to you and nobody else. I don't live on my own here, you know. My husband's quite capable of throwing out people's boyfriends, he's done it before – I'm only warning you. I lock up at ten.' Then she went away through a swing door, in a gust of cauliflower.

I heaved up my luggage, shut myself in, sat down on the bed. I had ten pounds left for tomorrow. Tomorrow I would have to find a way to live. That all too familiar knocking of the heart began again, and I pulled out a book, and tried to concentrate. But I was very tired. I was hungry, too, but I daren't spend any more. I wondered whether the tap to the ancient basin ran drinking water, but on closer inspection I saw it hadn't worked for years, the plumbing wasn't even connected. The bulb in the single, centre light was so low-powered that as soon as it was dark I had to stop reading. The sheets on the bed felt damp, and I lay fully dressed on top of the quilt with my jacket over my legs, and made pictures in the watermarks on the ceiling.

Hello there, Mum and Dad, so how are you feeling? Are you miserable, are you anxious? So am I.

Who says it was different in Victorian times? You didn't throw me out, but the result's the same. This is the barefoot-in-the-snow syndrome, with no one to turn to for help. I don't trust the welfare or the police. I come from a good home, my parents want me back – I oughtn't to be in a problem situation. These advantages have cut me off, even from my best friend.

Here lies Elizabeth the clever, the confident, the sort of girl you expect to go places. What am I going to do next? I want to find work and keep on with my studies after hours and enrol myself somewhere in September. I shall be sixteen by then. I shall also be a mother.

Just what is going to happen to me? It's not looking too brilliant at three o'clock in the morning. But I do go to sleep, on the thought that I shall stuff breakfast, to keep myself going through the day.

13

But they served a continental breakfast in that house – a roll and instant coffee; at any rate that was what they gave me, and I didn't dare to ask for more in case it was extra. The tray was carried in by a man in a pullover and shirtsleeves – the match for people's boyfriends I assumed. He stood staring out of the window while I ate, and when I had finished he came over to me and asked whether I was leaving right away.

'Yes.'

'Okay.' He whisked a pad out of his pocket, scribbled something, tore off the sheet and handed it to me. £15 was written on it.

'What's this?' I was so taken aback, I could hardly mumble out the words.

'That's what we charge for the top floor room.'

'But I paid yesterday!'

'Did you? Let's see your receipt. Sorry to ask, but we get all sorts, you'd be surprised.'

'She didn't give me one.'

'Who didn't?'

'The person who took the money.'

Then he wanted me to describe her, and rubbed his chin, and said it was a pity because she'd gone out for the day, so he'd have to ask me to stay on the premises until she came back – unless of course I liked to pay again, in which case, once she confirmed my story, he'd refund the money. He said he was sorry, but being in the bed and breakfast business had changed his attitude to human nature.

'But I have to go out, it's important!'

'That's all right, my dear, you go on, and I'll refund you

the fifteen, if she agrees you already paid it, no trouble at all.'

'But I haven't got another fifteen pounds!'

He looked at me with a little smile, as if he really couldn't believe that; but any fool could have told I was speaking the truth. So he said, 'How much *have* you got?'

'Ten.'

'That'll have to do then, won't it?' he said discontentedly. 'I'll just have to take your word for it. I'm soft, that's my trouble. I'll never be a millionaire, that's for sure!' He held out his hand, and much against my better judgement, with most desperate feelings, I gave him my last note. He said, 'She'll be back late afternoon, you can call in around sixish if you think you're entitled to a refund.' He sounded surly now; it was clear enough what he thought. He began stacking my breakfast things on to the tray. Obviously I'd upset him, added my quota to his disillusioned view of human nature. As he held the door open with his foot and grumpily disappeared, I suddenly realized that he hadn't given me a receipt for my ten pounds either. So I called after him, 'Please! Wait a minute!' But he didn't answer. The door swung shut. I hesitated for a few minutes, and then I picked up my bags and let myself out.

It was a beautiful morning, but that was the only good thing about it. I had about fifty pence and I spent it on a choc bar and a carton of milk. Very soon I was hungry again and not up to heaving my bags around, but what else could I do with them? I tried the girl in the sweetshop. 'Excuse me, but would you mind if I left these with you just for a couple of hours?' I could tell from her stare that it was no good, and my voice trailed away. After that I didn't ask again, until I went into the library for a rest; but the assistant explained that if it was a question of unattended luggage they always called the police. Then I sat between my bags with my arms round them, so there could be no mistake. I stared at the books without the least desire to open any of them, I felt utterly defeated and worn out. All morning I had been trying cafes and restaurants for waitressing or kitchen job, without any success; this afternoon it would have to be pubs. But I knew I wasn't likely to get anything. I wasn't neat enough, for a start. I hadn't been able to wash my hair for two days and it looked lank and greasy, and my expression was overanxious. My baggage didn't help. I wouldn't have wanted to employ me.

I tried several pubs. At last I went into the abbey and sat and stared at the ceiling. It would have been an artistic feast for anyone with a square meal inside them. After a while I felt calmer, and then I wondered at what historical point people had stopped turning to God as a solver of problems – what cataclysmic events had made a nonsense of the Divine Answer. I certainly wasn't the first pregnant girl to sit there wondering what the hell to do next, but some of them would have been praying. I wasn't. To me there was no point, and casting my mind over my class, I couldn't think of anyone except possibly Bella Rossi, who was Roman Catholic and went to Mass every Sunday in a black lace mantilla, who thought of prayer as more than a formality. I could think of plenty of people who wanted to go out and help the poverty-stricken to a fairer deal, but that was not related to religious conviction. That was philanthropy, no strings attached.

A man in a black robe crossed the nave in front of me and moved about among the choir stalls, arranging music probably. No doubt this place ran a hostel for destitutes and he would know about it. But it would be for down-and-outs, the real tramps, the alkies, and if I turned up it would be back to the social workers. I was trapped between Mum and the welfare. I remembered the hippies on the train, the girl in the hat who'd asked me to join them. I guessed they were making for the convoy which was more or less a fixture in Bath; I'd seen shots of it. I wasn't as proud as I had been yesterday, but I didn't intend to sink as low as that.

I rested there for a long time. I didn't find any answers, but there must have been something refreshing lurking between those old walls. For some illogical reason I walked out feeling more cheerful than I had since I left home – even my bags didn't seem so heavy. I saw that the sky was April blue and the air was full of pigeon noises in the paved square outside the abbey. I stopped to look up at the sculpted ladders and angels, some climbing, some falling. Morals were more distinct when they were made. In those days I would have been in danger of hellfire, I myself would have believed it. At least I didn't have that to contend with.

There were children rushing about in the square, chasing each other and the pigeons, and while I was staring at the angels, a little boy tripped on my book bag and came down with a crash. His sister, who had been threatening to beat him up, now burst into tears as well and bawled for Ma. I picked him up and he thumped me on the legs.

A good-looking girl got up from one of the seats round the square, and came languidly towards us. 'Oh Sasha, are you hurt?' she said without much interest. He hugged her knees and wept into her coat. 'I'm sorry,' I said. I was crimson with embarrassment.

'What for?'

'It was my bag he fell on.'

'He should have been looking where he was going.'

Her voice was light and attractive. Now she was close I saw that she was a good deal older than I expected – thirty at least; she wore a lot of make-up and she was beautifully dressed. She was so languid, it seemed almost more than she could manage, to comfort her child; but her dark-blue eyes with short, mascara'd lashes did not fit the image. They were acute, observant.

'Come on, Sash,' she said. 'You can choose the buns for tea.'

They started to move away. I had a sudden inspiration. I blurted out, 'Excuse me, but I suppose you don't. . . . Do you happen to know anybody who needs help in the house? Children, some cooking – that sort of thing?'

She turned and looked at me again and said simply, 'Of course. We all do.'

'What I mean is – I'm looking for a job.'

It was to me as if, suddenly, everything in the square – tourists, mothers, children, even the pigeons – hung fire for an instant. If only she knew how much was at stake!

She said, 'I suppose I might have some suggestions. You can come back to tea if you like.'

We set off across the square. As we passed the group where she had been sitting, there were whispers and somebody laughed, and my face burned as I felt myself scrutinized.

They lived in one of the streets above the abbey and the river. The way was steep and we hardly talked; I had enough to do to keep up. The little girl spun in and out of shop doorways, lagged behind to look at something, raced on ahead. Her mother never bothered to take her hand, only called out sharply, 'Fleur!' if there was a road to cross, with Sasha trotting, holding on to her coat. Sometimes he scowled at me.

We reached a terrace of elegant little houses railed in from the pavement, with steps down to the basement, up to the front door. Fleur was already jigging outside number nine, and her mother unlocked the door, and we went in. I dumped my bags in the tiny hall, and followed the others down to the kitchen. It reminded me at once of the Robinsons', although it was all-over pretty and had cost far more. There was the same casual air about the place, that made me feel at home. The children helped themselves to yoghurt out of the fridge, while their mother threw her coat over a chair and put the kettle on.

'I'm Nina Burman. What's your name?'

'Elizabeth. Elizabeth Davis.'

'And you're how old?'

'Sixteen.'

'Of course.' I couldn't tell if she believed me. She filled the teapot, reached down mugs, opened a packet of wholegrain sliced bread, put butter and honey on the table. I stood there trying not to drool. 'You realize that people are going to ask you why you've left home; any responsible employer will want to know. Sit down, help yourself to bread and butter.'

My hand shook, spreading a slice. I ate as slowly as I could; even then Fleur commented, 'She's hungry, isn't she?'

'Yes, my sweet, she is.' Nina was drinking her tea, holding the mug with both hands, observing me. She waited politely until I had finished and then asked, 'Well? What happened?'

'I want to be independent.' It sounded feeble enough.

'Don't we all! And here you are gobbling away for dear life – go on, take some more, there's plenty of bread in the house. Have you got anywhere to sleep tonight?'

No point in lying about that. 'No.'

'So I can hardly turn you out, can I? A girl of your age. Do you call that being independent?'

Silence in the kitchen.

'Now I'll tell you what I'm looking for – more tea?' she asked, filling my mug. 'I want another pair of hands to turn on the washer and the vacuum cleaner, another pair of feet to take the children to and from nursery. I have a career lying about somewhere, and it would be nice to pick it up again. I also have a spare room, which would be handy for someone with nowhere to go. Such a person would have to live as family, which doesn't mean being out all night—'

'Well, obviously—'

'Don't interrupt! I was about to say I'm prepared to take the risk with you, I flatter myself I'm a good judge of character. Whether Clay will agree is another thing. I'll just have to try to persuade him.'

I washed up the tea things to prove I was useful. After that, Fleur and Sasha showed me the house, but all the time I was on the alert for the coming of Clay, and I couldn't help feeling apprehensive when I heard his feet in the hall – not that they sounded specially loud or decisive. I was so afraid he wouldn't go along with this situation, that his wife had virtually picked up a girl to help. But I needn't have worried; when we met I had the feeling, from his baffled but unsurprised expression, that I wasn't the first stranger he had found at home in his house.

He interviewed me – or tried to – in the elegant drawing room on the first floor. He was slim with brown hair and regular features slightly marred by a permanent frown, perhaps indicating the strain of life with Nina, who was there too, reclining on a sofa.

'This is Elizabeth,' she announced. 'We know she's sixteen, and she says her surname is Davis, and she's left home because she wants to be independent. Say something,' she commanded me.

'I like your house. It's really nice.' It was the only thing I could think of to say. I was feeling amazingly awkward.

'Are you in trouble with the police or anything?' asked Clay.

'Darling! Just because she likes the house, it doesn't mean she's a burglar!'

'No, but I have to ask her. I'm sure she appreciates that.'

'But it's such a *stupid* question! If she's a bad lot she could spin you any old yarn – how would you find it out? Be reasonable! You're talking as if you could afford a proper nanny. The point is that I am not frightfully well after having my babies rather late in life, and it would be marvellous for me to have some help with Sash and Fleur.' She turned to me. 'Did they show you your room?'

'You mean the little one at the top?'

'Well, it's not very large, and I'm afraid it does need a bit of decorating, but you may feel like doing that later on. You'll eat with us, of course. It's rather scatter-brained here but you're welcome to anything you can find in the fridge. How well do you know Bath?'

'Not very.'

'You'll love it! It's so pretty, and there's heaps to do, but you want to study, don't you?'

'Why should she?' from Clay.

'Don't *pounce*, darling! One of her bags is full of books.' No flies on Nina. 'Pour me a whisky, I want to drink to Elizabeth.' She stretched, catlike among the cushions. 'May your stay be long and happy! I daresay it'll all work out well,' she added, reflectively. 'You'll probably live with us for years. In the end you'll marry from here, a handsome middle-aged woman, with Sash and Fleur as your bridal attendants.'

'Don't be ridiculous, pet,' muttered Clay, embarrassed.

I just thought myself unbelievably lucky. What a fool! I was in for a rude shock.

14

Day one. Seven-thirty call from Clay, who thumps my door without speaking or bringing in a cup of tea – not that I expect it. I have to force myself to leave my narrow bed (even though it has been moved up here because the springs have gone), wash and dress and join the family at breakfast. Their allure has worn thin overnight; Clay is in a rush, Nina is grumpy and pasty-faced without make-up, the kids are obstreperous. Clay leaves for his work in an interior design business, and I accompany Nina to the nursery school where Fleur and Sasha spend the day. We return to number nine, picking up some bits of shopping on the way which she allows me to carry, and I pay attention while she explains the working of the washing machine and dishwasher. She leaves me to load them and monopolizes the bathroom for an hour, finally swans off for the day looking a million dollars having reminded me to tidy the kids' beds and collect them at three. Incidentally I detect a certain expertise in her organization of myself that suggests I am not the first young sucker to occupy that handy attic room.

I have finished by midday so I make myself a cottage cheese sandwich (the contents of the fridge, so freely offered, are and remain skimpy), and go out, locking the door as instructed and realizing, too late, that I have left my key inside the house. I eat my sandwich in the library and spend two hours there, but it is not very fruitful as all such places have their own layout and I'm not familiar with this one. I pick up the children on time, mingling with the other drudges and unemployed mothers. Then finding Nina still out and the house impenetrably locked, Sasha whines and

Fleur plays hopscotch on the pavement until she turns up and lets us in. I'm left to make the tea while she treats herself to a long bath and early night. Enter Clay, and he spends most of the evening in her room. It is for me to supervise the winkie bath and bed. Luckily they know where everything is, and apart from Sasha splitting his lip on the washbasin, they aren't much trouble. They ask for a story, and I am trailing upstairs with a book, when I can't help overhearing part of a conversation in the parental bedroom.

'Don't overdo it, pet – she won't stay.'

'Rubbish, she's thrilled to be here! Why, don't you think she's getting good value? We could let that room for eighty – a hundred pounds a week –'

As time passed, I came to the conclusion that they would have done better to let the room and take the money. Clay's shoes were down at heel and his suit needed pressing; his business wasn't as lucrative as Nina would have liked, and he had a hang-up about this, as well as her health after bearing his children, as well as etc. He blamed himself too much, the general scruffiness of the family wasn't all his fault. The children had a motherless appearance. Their hair needed trimming, and although their clothes had prestigious name tickets, they were obviously secondhand, because Nina never bothered to alter them, and didn't care whether they fitted properly. All her attention was lavished on herself, and that was why I was necessary to her.

She couldn't afford to pay me anything, but she was ready with compliments if she thought I was getting resentful. 'You are wonderful. I simply can't imagine how we managed before you came,' and, 'You're intelligent, aren't you? I don't have to *explain* everything.' These remarks don't look so good on paper, but they sounded genuine, brought out on the spur of the moment as if straight from the heart. And (as it turned out, significantly), 'You're discreet, aren't you? You don't *chat*.'

'I haven't got anyone to chat to.'

'Oh dear, do you mean you're lonely? We can't have that! I must invite some nice people for you to meet.'

But she never did.

And although I could read her like a book, she was so charming that I couldn't help being flattered by her unstinted praise, or enjoying the occasions when she pretended to have a headache and stayed all morning in bed. Then I would carry up coffee for two on a tray to the dimness of her room, and our conversation would be, appropriately, more intimate. She never wanted to hear about my life, although there were times when I would have told her quite a lot. She talked about her childhood, how glad she had been to leave home, how misunderstood by her parents. I heard all about Clay's courtship of her, his long and expensive pursuit. Too obviously she had sold herself to the highest bidder, and too obviously he loved her to distraction, if that means that she distracted him from everything else. Poor old Clay.

The children were now very sweet with me and I got fond of them. ('You're brilliant with kids. It's a gift. Sash and Fleur simply adore you.') In fact, if only there'd been a chance of any money, I could have stayed put for their sakes. In my optimistic moments I fantasized about being lent a pram, a cot, allowed to share my attic room with a baby. In reality I was increasingly anxious about how I was going to make out. My savings were melting away; besides the small things everyone needs to keep replacing, like tissues and shampoo, I had to buy meat to supplement Nina's milk-based economy.

But what worried me more than anything was the impossibility of studying on my own. I missed the discipline of class, I needed the stimulus of competition, other brains round me. How often I sat in that library, accomplishing nothing, and could have cried with frustration when the time came to trail back up the hill to fetch the children! Once home at number nine, there were the chores to do – nothing heavy, but time-consuming. I never sat with Nina and Clay – *she* wouldn't have cared, but I didn't want to wreck his evening. So I'd go to bed early, full of good intentions – and fall asleep before I could tackle anything.

My pregnancy is making me brain-dead, Mum – do you hear that? Remember all those results you and Dad were so proud of, all my plans for the future? *Plans*? *Certainty*! A sparkling conveyance just waiting for me to take my place, destination SUCCESS ASSURED. So what happened? I've been sidetracked, I haven't been able to obtain the necessary tickets, and (let's face facts) I've missed the bus. It's gone off without me, just as you said it would.

My golden goal has – vanished. Life is a bit bleak without it, just as you said it would be. Right again, darling!

The days passed quickly – weeks – a month. One morning Nina said to me, 'You know I think you've put on weight since you came here.'

She watched my face flame.

'Goodness, don't worry! It suits you. You look really well, and never a spot. When I was sixteen I was covered in spots!'

That was hard to believe.

The weather set fair and I bought myself some Indian clothes in a sale – a full skirt and sleeveless top, a loose-fitting dress printed in pastel colours. It was true that I looked bigger, but not pregnant – perhaps slightly thick sideways, but the gathers were concealing. Sash sitting on my knee suddenly demanded, 'What's that jumping inside of you?'

'Indigestion.' I willed him to forget it, but as soon as he saw his mother he blurted out, 'Beff has got ingestion jumping inside of her.'

Nina laughed at him and said, 'That's what ladies get, Sash.'

'Is it a dying disease?' asked Fleur without raising her eyes from her painting.

'No, my sweet, it is not.'

God knows I must have looked embarrassed, and I

expected some sort of cross-examination later. But it didn't come.

By this time I'd met Archie. I don't remember the exact day it happened, during my little space of free time, between the hours of eleven and three, when I often poked into the junk shops, the dark interiors where they sold anything from hat pins to rocking horses. Archie's business was books. He was friendly and conversational, a good deal older than me, with wiry grey hair and very bright blue eyes. He never asked questions but he was a good listener, which has to be a rare combination. He seemed a person one could trust.

Instant heart-throb? I was lonely, that's all. He was interesting too; if nobody else read his books, he did, and he knew a lot. Heaven knows what he saw in me. What's this? Do I mean *me*, *Elizabeth* – top of the class at the start of this account?

After a while we started meeting for lunch, once or twice a week. We would have spaghetti or a salad. Those dates were oases in my life; once they started, I gave up my search for a midday washing-up job. It was hopeless anyway, the hours I could manage never suited anybody. What was I going to do? Lack of realism! In-built certainty that it would sort itself out! And it does, you know. If you don't steer yourself, sooner or later Fate will take over.

There are so many tiny, in themselves insignificant parts to Fate, any amount of clues we ought to spot before the thunderbolt, the so-called act of God, plummets down and shatters everything. Mine probably began long before Archie invited me to a jazz concert. It was the first evening off I'd asked for, and it simply didn't occur to me that Nina, who was always taking advantage of me as permanent baby-sitter, would be funny about it. What an error! Her face clouded immediately.

'Oh, *God*. Does this mean you're going to be gadding about from now on? I thought it was too good to last!'

'Of course not! I didn't think you'd mind.'

'It isn't that I *mind*. I'm just too well acquainted with people who use me like a hotel and stay out till all hours. I was hoping you weren't going to be like that.' A pause – she was waiting for me to say I wouldn't go. She went on spitefully, 'Who are you going out with? That shabby little book man, I suppose. Clay saw you with him.' I was red but still I said nothing. She tried another tack, determined to get her own way – Fleur had more finesse. 'It happens to be Clay's and my anniversary. Still, that doesn't matter, you weren't to know, that's not your fault.' Careless mistake! I remembered the anniversary, soon after I came to the house – who but Nina could have forgotten it? Red roses, champagne, the lot. 'All right, Elizabeth,' sighing. 'How poor Sashy and Fleur will hate it, I don't expect they'll sleep a wink all night.'

After which it hardly seemed worth going; but I went.

It was the first hiccup in our relationship, and I have to admit it upset me. It was impossible to live in that house without putting Nina's happiness at the top of the list. I don't know why. There were several gloomy days to endure while I waited for her to call me 'Beff' again, Sasha's name for me which had spread through the family. Had I known it, my attempts to get back on a friendly footing were simply adding weight to the thunderbolt.

Archie never rang or called at number nine. There had been an unlucky incident over some books that Clay thought valuable, which Nina considered it her duty to tell me about, in case I was *getting involved*. So when I turned up at our Italian place and he couldn't make it because of a last-minute appointment, he left a message for me with the cook. That was okay. I stuffed chili con carne and had a Coke compliments of the management, and left the bistro feeling cheerful. And there on the corner was somebody selling flowers, and it was a beautiful, sparkling day.

So I bought a bunch of pinks, and the person added some gyp – there are days when everything looks brilliant, and people add for pleasure without being asked, or paid. When I got back I went down to the kitchen and washed out a vase, and arranged them; and then I went upstairs intending to put them in Nina's bedroom, for a peace offering.

I expected the room to be empty. But Nina was in the bed, and the man with her was not Clay. They must have had a breathless minute when they heard my key in the door, another while I climbed the stairs. They were frozen into one attitude, Nina looking over his shoulder, white as the sheet but for two spots of crimson on her cheeks.

I closed the door and went back to the kitchen and placed the vase of flowers very exactly in the centre of the table. Then I put on some water for coffee. It wasn't until I heard the lid jittering against the kettle that I realised I was trembling.

The front door banged, and almost at once a pair of elastic-sided shoes and tidy trouser ends sped the top width of that basement window. Nina would come down in a minute. When she came, I was sitting drinking my mug of coffee, perfectly calm.

'Beff,' she said – instant return to the old pedestal! 'Beff! I thought you said you were going to be out for lunch.'

'Sorry sorry, I didn't know it was important.'

Significant pause.

'I suppose you're very shocked.'

I was going to say no, automatically, but a moment's thought turned it to, 'I suppose I am, a bit.'

She said nothing while she made herself coffee, and then she took the chair opposite mine, and our eyes met for the first time since the bedroom. She looked – different; and it struck me that for the first time I was seeing her without a mask.

'Do you want me to explain?'

'Not particularly.'

She suddenly laughed. 'You sound so cross! Almost as if you were – jealous!'

I didn't like that. I said roughly, 'He's been here to dinner, hasn't he? I've met him several times. One of Clay's friends.'

'That's right. Why, do you think it would be better if he came off the street?'

But it was all rushing in on me. I was thinking how much she was loved, of the elegant, disorderly bedroom (Nina never put anything away), of his weight on Clay's side of the mattress, of her not even bothering to change the sheets. . . . I couldn't bear to sit there any longer. I got up and made a business of washing and drying my mug. Nina hardly ever smoked, but now she lit a cigarette, and exhaling, narrowing her eyes against the smoke, she watched me.

I looked at the kitchen clock. 'I'd better go and fetch the children.'

'Don't make excuses, there's plenty of time. You're feeling sore for Clay, aren't you?'

'Yes.'

She suddenly ground out her half-smoked fag and jumped up from the chair. 'Come upstairs a minute.'

I followed without any idea what was in her mind. It seemed odd that she was more animated than I had ever known her, while I felt miserable. She went into her bedroom without the slightest self-consciousness, where loomed the Bed with tumbled sheets – I tried not to look at it. She opened the cupboard where her clothes were hanging, soft materials, glowing colours, worked through them impatiently, searching for something. It was a coat she finally extracted, an oatmeal mohair with matching braid round the collarless neck and three-quarter-length sleeves.

'Here,' she said. 'Try it. I promise you it's hardly been worn. This colour does horrible things to my skin.'

A bribe.

'Go on,' she repeated, not understanding. 'It'll look fabulous on you. I want you to have it.'

'What for?' I said. I hardly knew how to get out the words. 'Are you afraid I'll tell Clay?'

'Of course not! You wouldn't do a thing like that!'

But she wasn't taking any chances.

I turned and went out. I was late for the children and had to hurry up the hill. I suppose she put the coat away. She didn't mention it again.

15

'I've got to go.

'It isn't her sex life, whatever she thinks. I couldn't care less what she does and anyway it's not my business. I'm sorry for Clay, but then he's a wimp. Surely he ought to know what she's up to, she doesn't take much trouble to hide it. I think it's disgusting to carry on in the same bed, but she'd say what's the difference, which is logical enough. No, the trouble is it's completely blitzed our relationship. I find double meanings in everything, like this morning when she asked me if I'd be in for lunch; what else can I think?

'I hate seeing her with Clay. He's so besotted and can't see that she might even love him if he beat her up. I'm pretty sure he knows it's happening but he won't admit it, he can't face it. It's a load of lies all round and bad for the children – they're lucky they've got each other.'

Archie was listening, as we walked along the canal. The summer was unbelievably warm so far, cloudless day after cloudless day, and he worried about the greenhouse effect, but I simply enjoyed it. In fact these were now my only enjoyable times. Nina had given up the idea of getting round me. I got the cold shoulder instead, and her shoulders were colder than most people's. I knew it was silly, but it was making my life unbearable when we were boxed in together in the pretty house. The other three took their cue from her and Clay avoided me, while Sasha and Fleur got naughty and even nasty. They sensed at once that my days were numbered – oh, I was not by any means their first expendable au pair! This hurt more than anything – the ease with which they forgot the stories, the sweets and little toys, and ditched their friend.

'The children will grow up like her, they haven't a chance. Add two more cold, shallow people to the numbers in the world. It's a pity they're good-looking, they'll do more harm.

'Yesterday they were discussing the holidays; one of the grand-mothers is renting a cottage at the seaside and they're going there for a month. Nina's already made it clear to all that she'd sooner go abroad, but she says it'll save money. She comes out with these unmentionable things. Sash wanted to know if I was going too but she said I was *making my own arrangements*. So I'd better, as soon as possible.'

After this we had a constructive discussion about jobs, and Archie said he'd keep his ear to the ground. I felt reasonably confident when he was there. But when he'd ridden off on his motorbike to go and look at somebody's books, a thin but jaunty figure, I climbed wearily to the nursery school feeling quite sick with fright. Pregnant Girl Starves on Pavement, I imagined the headline. Desperate Elizabeth Russell (alias Davis), 15, was in care last night after being picked up in the last stages of filth and degradation by Bath Social Services. The girl, until recently posing as a 16-year-old au pair at the home of Mrs Nina Burman, 37, struggled to get away but was too weak. Her parents have been informed. Mrs Burman comments, We knew Beff had a past but it seemed irrelevant to ask questions.

The family was going away for July, which was only three weeks off. At school they'd be in the middle of exams – not mocks, but the real thing. Ann would do well, and I wished I could have sent her a good-luck card. Good luck was what I needed myself. I seemed to have slipped into a state of total anxiety. That night I knocked out another Mental Message to Mum (the knocking being the beating of my heart) – how much does it matter not having all those medical checks you read about? What happens if my little but ever increasing Burden is suffering from some horrible deficiency? After a slow start, he's getting really active, hardly an hour passes but he hammers for attention. Is he a psychopath or just four-legged? I'm having a lot of worries about this side of him – a phase, probably. If I was Chrissie you'd be holding my hand and being comforting, plus you'd have showered him with presents, which would be extremely welcome in my situation. Only ten weeks to go before The Birth you tried so hard to prevent – what made you think you had any right to interfere? I am genuinely curious to know your reasoning (if any). I still find it totally immoral, amoral or unmoral (discuss the differences, girls, in three clear sentences, not forgetting to write your name at the head of the paper).

It was next morning that Nina said, out of the blue, 'It would be a good thing if you started looking for another job, Elizabeth.'

Damn.

'I was leaving anyway.'

'While you are still able to work,' she went on, smoothly, as if I hadn't spoken. I stared. I felt the hot colour rising from my low-cut top.

'When is it due?'

But of course, she'd known all along! She'd had this weapon poised, like the sword of Damocles, over my head, surveying it from time to time with one of her enigmatic smiles; finally, a twitch of the string and I was annihilated. She studied my stupefied countenance, and actually laughed. 'You must think I'm a fool! It was the obvious thing; and now, of course, it *is* very obvious. I'd sooner the children didn't tell their friends. We try to keep out of that league game.'

I didn't answer; in fact, now I come to think of it, I never spoke to her again. I went upstairs and started cramming my belongings into my bags. I was stiff all over with rage, even the sympathetic Burden went hard and still, as if he was holding his breath. I bundled myself downstairs and out by the front. Nina had made herself invisible. I slammed the door. Too late I remembered a couple of beef sandwiches that were mine in the fridge. She'd probably eat them for lunch. I hauled my things as far as the shop where Archie worked. There was a little public garden with seats close by, and I turned in there for a rest. When I was calmer, and had thought a bit, I crossed the road and entered the bookshop.

Archie seemed to run the place single-handed, I never saw another assistant in there; but then it wasn't exactly thronged with buyers. I didn't know, and never found out, how he scraped a living. He was pleased to see me, which was nice. 'Hi, Liz! A bit early for you, isn't it?'

'I'm here as a customer.'

'Great! What are you buying?'

'Selling.' I opened the book bag, took out my text books one by one and ranged them on the counter. 'They're all up to date, current syllabus. Could you sell them for me?'

'Well, yes,' he said, opening one, glancing through it. Then I noticed the school's name stamped in purple ink on the fly leaf. He looked from that to my face.

'How much could you get for them?'

'A bit. The English stuff isn't worth anything.' This was tattered paperbacks of the novels and plays we'd covered in the course. 'There's always a demand from people who've had to leave school early for some reason, but want to carry on studying.' He paused for a comment from me but I said nothing. He went on, 'If you've bothered to cart them around all this time, what do you want to sell them for?'

'Cash.'

'They won't make that much difference to your budget. Fifteen quid at the most; that's being optimistic.'

'Fifteen quid is food for several days. I've got to eat.'

'You've walked out then?'

'Yes.'

The person who had been browsing in a corner of the shop

now pushed his volume back on the shelf and went out. I said, 'There, I've cost you a sale.'

'Not to worry, he'll be back.' Archie was never cast down by the people who used him as a library. 'Have you got anywhere to stay?'

'No, and I've spent nearly all my money. It's all my fault, but she was so charming to start with. That sort of person – they somehow cut the ground from under your feet.'

He looked quickly at me, and at his watch, and he said, 'I may as well shut for lunch. Give us your baggage.' He stowed it under the counter, and we left the shop. We walked down to the canal, our steps turning naturally in the same direction. We sat down on the grass. I stared across at the opposite bank and said, 'I'm expecting a baby.' It was something he had to know. I hated telling him, I'd been putting it off for weeks. Now the words came out in this somehow old-fashioned phrase, when ordinarily I would just have said, 'I'm pregnant.' But I didn't want to shock this gentleman who was my friend.

'Oh dear.'

How feeble that looks, written down. Let me explain the implications of those two words. First, he was sorry, because it had happened, and he knew that it must have been an accident. So he spoke gently, sympathetically. I also saw at once that however obvious Nina had said it now was and always had been, it was news to him. He wasn't a person to draw that sort of conclusion. Lastly, his sympathy somehow covered my baby as well – a tough start, he might have said, oh dear.

Are you listening, Mum? Here's a lesson for you, and Archie probably never read an article on teenagers in his life!

After that neither of us spoke for a bit. I was chasing back the lump in my throat with the sandwiches he was sharing with me.

'When are you having it?'

'Two months or so.'

We sat side by side like two married people, not touching, staring in the same direction.

'Anyway you would have had to leave number nine.'

'Oh yes, I was going. I couldn't have stayed there much longer. You know how I hated it.'

'You're going to carry on working?'

'I'll have to. I'll start looking this afternoon. It ought to be easier to find something, now I'm not tied down at all hours.'

'Could be.'

'It's difficult to know what to do.'

'Yes,' he said. 'It is.'

'It isn't that I haven't thought about it. I think about it most of the time. At first I tried to get rid of it, but that didn't work out. So now I'm having it but I haven't done any of the things you're meant to do and I'm not registered or booked in or anything. I just can't face it. I hate categories. I don't want to be a Schoolgirl Mum or At Risk or In Care. I'm not going into a hostel full of stupid girls giggling and shrieking about their boyfriends. I suppose I've gone along hoping it'll sort itself out. But it isn't going to, is it? It's going to happen. I don't know what to do.'

Archie reached out and took my hand. It was the first time he had done this, he was the most un-physical friend. I don't know how long we sat there on the grass, holding hands, staring across that slow strip of oily water. Finally he said, 'I'd better get back to the shop,' and we stood up.

We didn't talk on the way. As he unlocked the shop he said, 'I'll take care of your bags if you like. Call back some time around five, and tell me how you got on.'

Perhaps while I'm job hunting, successfully as it turned out, there is an opportunity to enlarge my description of Archie. He was as I've said grey-haired and thin, not springy fit like Dad, but more of an underfed thinness. If Nina called him shabby that must have been because his clothes were old; he was always tidy and clean. His face was somewhat skull-shaped because of the prominence of the bones and his eyes were the kindest I have ever seen. I never discovered anything about his background, he never spoke of it, but I had the impression that he was or had been close to his mother, and that his father had either left or died when he was young. I don't think he was ever married; he wasn't gay. For one reason or another, he needed to stand free. He was reticent, and although I got to know *him* as well as I've ever known anyone, I knew very little *about* him. There were zones in his life that he was not prepared to share.

'Any luck?' he called as I reappeared in the narrow doorway.

'Yes!'

'Living in?'

'No, but she thought she knew of a room. I've to go back at six. It's at Gilda's, waitressing and washing up. They need someone over the holiday period.'

'Will that bring in enough to live on?'

'Yes, if I do the hours. It's only one-fifty an hour.'

'Slave labour!'

He was right. We sat over coffee at Gilda's and I found out how much the available room would cost. I did the sums in my head while he was still getting out a pencil and paper: if I worked nine hours a day, seven days a week, I could afford the room plus keep myself plus, perhaps, save a tiny bit towards the baby. It was crazy. Anyway, Gilda didn't open on Sundays.

'I can offer you a bed,' said Archie suddenly.

I stared at him. Under my gaze, he started to blush.

'It's a double room,' he explained. 'I mean, there's two beds. What I mean is, I'm not propositioning you.'

'But you don't—'

'It's there if you want it.'

Gilda came and took our cups and wiped our table. We got up. 'Yes, please,' I said.

I'd never seen Archie's place, but I knew he lived on one of the main roads out of Bath. He wheeled out his bike which he kept behind the bookshop, and made me wear his helmet. We strapped on the bags and set off, precariously; he wasn't the world's steadiest rider, and turning across the street in the rush hour was a terrifying experience. The house where he rented a room was detached, Victorian, one in a line of huge crumbling mansions all divided up, or empty awaiting development. But there was a good expanse of railed-in paving between the traffic and the portico, and once inside it was surprisingly quiet. Archie kept his bike in the hall. He grappled with it up the steps and through the door. His relationship with it was always more or less frustrated; a balloon would have suited him better.

He lived in the large front room on the right. I'd often wondered what his version of home would be like, it was so difficult to imagine him against a settled background. If people are made up of elements, his was entirely air. I was surprised to find all neat, and academic. Quantities of books were not unexpected, but they were arranged on shelves, and there were objects that he had probably inherited, such as an Art Nouveau standard lamp in the shape of a lily, and a metal trunk painted to look like wood. The curtains were dull red and must have come originally from an even larger room, for though these windows were tall, there was plenty to spare bunched under them. I stood looking round, taken aback, and flattered because I felt that all this was a dimension of Archie which in ordinary circumstances he would have kept apart. It was a proof of fondness for me, and as I write this I am comforted.

Meanwhile he was unhitching my bags, and now he carried them in, and placed them side by side by the second bed, a low divan covered with scarlet cloth. Then he said, 'You make a cup of tea, and I'll go and talk to the Jellybean.'

A bamboo partition concealed Archie's cooking arrangements, but it took me a while to track down the milk which was in the fridge in the passage, and by that time he had returned with Angela Behan, the landlady. We shook hands.

I heard later that she was a carpet dealer, but she can't have had much trade; she lived on her rents and drank too much. This showed in her purplish complexion and little wary eyes, which got bolder under the influence. Her hair was thick and brown, and she wore an ethnic skirt with a black sleeveless tee shirt, old beige sandals and several strings of painted wooden beads. She may have had other clothes, but I never saw them. I liked her because she was nice to me. She would have done anything for Archie.

She lent us a screen to put round my bed, and Archie let me have the tin trunk for my things. I took out the dress Dad had bought me in Crete, and draped it over the ugly screen to make a splash of colour. When I had finished unpacking I came out and joined them where they were sitting in cane chairs in the window bay, with the potted plants. Archie was very much a rush-and-cane man, as I might have guessed if I'd thought about it. We talked for a while and then I retired to bed. I lay on my back with my hands linked behind my head, on the cushion that served as pillow and smelt of old books, and watched the room gradually darken, the figures in the window dwindle from flesh and blood to silhouette. I was happy, more happy than I'd been for months; and more peaceful than I'd ever been in my life. I had a feeling of *having arrived intact*. Goodness knows why.

16

Predictably, Gilda's was slavery from nine until six, but she paid promptly, and the wages included a midday meal, which I could choose from the untouched-by-human-foot products of her kitchen. I also got perks in the form of unsold grub (repeat, grub) at the end of the day. These treats I carried home for Archie and me. I made him take twenty pounds a week for my bed, but I know for a fact that he gave it all to Jelly. Thinking about it afterwards, I believe he had a horror of any kind of hoarding, which he saw not as freedom, but as a ball and chain. He liked enough – several bottles of wine in the bamboo rack, an occasional steak; and he always paid his bills when they came in (James Archer, the envelopes called him – not Archibald Blank). But he was cautious about accumulating things, apart from the books which clung and multiplied. Maybe that was the reason why he wasn't a family man. It wouldn't have extended him, it would have worn him away.

His attitude to his surroundings was bizarre. Nothing was accidental, all was calculated down to the potted plants, which were, he believed, beneficial to the health of a person forced to live in a city. Once he was used to my company, he told me that he was 'glad the divan has come into its own'. He had lived alone so much that each object was invested with heightened significance. Sometimes he felt that spacious room so breathless, he had to open the door to let the pressure out.

I was now part of his routine, and this included a mug of early morning tea in my bed, when he was still dressed in striped pyjamas and smelt of toothpaste and shaving cream. I don't know how he would have reacted if I had persisted in the slovenly habits I'd fallen into at Nina's – not making my bed, for instance. But I am orderly by nature and I much preferred his way of life. He went out quite a lot, which was unexpected, and he was usually late coming back. After heaving the bike into the house, which never failed to wake me and probably most of the other tenants, he would creep into our room. Then if he was in the mood he would say 'Liz?' in his quietest voice, and if I was too I would answer, 'Mmmm?' in the voice of one rousing. 'Do you fancy a mug of Horlicks?' 'Yes, okay, thanks, that would be nice.' And we might make a midnight feast of it, with sardines on toast, or a sandwich. But he never talked about where he'd been, or invited me along. Sometimes he took his accordion with him, folded to look like a suitcase. From the hours he kept I guessed he played in a pub, but he never did at home.

We had the ground floor to ourselves. A couple of school teachers lived above, something to do with further education, plus a bloke with a flat-top haircut and three earrings on one side who worked as a chef. The second floor was shared by four typists, which left the attics and the basement for Jellybean; I think it must have been mostly the attics because whenever I met her she was coming downstairs. One evening she knocked on our door. Archie was out – she'd have known that from the absence of his bike. I opened, and saw at once that she had been drinking – her eyes were poked right in and her puce face was freshly flushed. As she pushed past me I got a blast of her usual patchouli fragrance as well as the indefinable spiritous (not -ed, not -ual) aroma that somehow she never managed to extinguish. She was breathing heavily, so that the beads rose and fell on the swell of the tee shirt. When she spoke her voice throbbed, several tones deeper than usual, and I pinned down the aroma as gin.

'Is He the Father of your Child?'

'No way!'

The hundred per cent genuine astonishment in my voice

must have been convincing. She stared at me, reading my mind with her tiny eyes. Then she moved heavily to the window and sat down, and I made her a coffee. When she had finished it, she went away. That question must have been torturing her for days. She never referred to it again.

There was a fireworks display, and I went with Archie to watch. We walked to the park and stood in the crowd in the soft night, holding hands so as not to lose each other, under the gently rustling trees. The show was late in starting, and people kept coming, so we were surrounded by the expectant murmur, the eager audience distorted by the lights and shadows of the city at night. Several times I thought I recognized various faces which a movement or a breath of wind turned into strangers. 'Look over there, Archie, isn't that—' but the person vanished before I could get out a name.

There came without any warning a searing rush, which snatched a gasp from the crowd, as the first bouquet of rockets shot into the stars. We were all instantaneously floodlit – and it was then I saw the Burmans, Nina with a jacket over her shoulders, Fleur spellbound for once, Sash riding Clay. The light faded as the flowers died and the coloured sparks fell back, slowly, slowly over our upturned faces. When I looked again, Nina and Clay and the children had melted into different people, or disappeared altogether.

When it was over we walked home eating fish and chips, and I went to bed while Archie made Horlicks for me and poured himself a glass of wine. He liked a glass when he was preparing something, it was oil to his activities, and he always hummed when he was busy. By the time he had turned on the lily lamp, closed the curtains and watered the plants, I was sitting up in bed in the shirt I kept for sleeping in. We had worked out a way of living side by side which was private for each of us, and highly civilized.

That evening, while we were drinking together, he shattered the companionable silence by suddenly asking,

'What are you going to do with the baby?' It was the first time he'd mentioned it since I told him I was pregnant. I didn't know what to say. He enlarged the question. 'Are you keeping it, or having it adopted?'

'I don't know. I'm not sure.'

'What are you going to call it?'

'I don't know.'

'Is it a girl or a boy?'

'I told you, I haven't had any of those checks.'

'So it could be twins.'

'I suppose so.' Something occurred to me and I added, 'Mum was a twin.'

'Where are you having it?'

By this time my cheeks were red. I said angrily, 'I suppose you think I'm very childish and irresponsible. I'll have it in hospital, of course.'

'That's all right then. I don't see Jelly as a midwife, and I always faint at the sight of blood.'

I hesitated, and then I thought I might as well tackle the next question since we were on the subject. 'What about afterwards? You won't want it here.'

'You could bring it back till you found something else.' He gazed vaguely round. 'I don't quite know where we'd put it. In there perhaps, if we propped the lid open; it wouldn't be the first baby to start life in a trunk. If it was twins we'd be a bit pushed for space.'

'That's really nice of you, Archie,' I said with warmth. 'I'll see it doesn't cry.'

'I'm sure it won't,' he said.

After this conversation I spent a lot of my free time trailing round Mothercare and Boots and M & S, fingering the baby things. One day I took the plunge and bought some tiny vests. Size one, they said. They were small, small. My fingers fitted in the little sleeves. Fortunately they were made of pure cotton; Archie had strong feelings about this.

'But *nappies*, Archie! I'll have to get disposables. We'll never be able to dry the other sort!'

'We'll manage.' He with his paper, I in my head worked out that it would actually save money to buy a tumble dryer. We found one secondhand. Jellybean contributed, and we installed it in the ground floor bathroom, for the use of the three of us.

Jelly was slowly knitting a tight suit of undyed natural wool. It smelt of lanolin and felt prickly. I bought some bits of Liberty lawn and made little shirts. Even allowing for mistakes, they were nicer than anything ready-made, and soon I got expert at tiny stitches and button holes, pleats and bias binding. I sewed in the evenings, at the table in the window. I'd never played with dolls, I think they're usually revolting, but I used to like dressing them. Now I enjoyed taking it up again.

I am a perfectionist when it comes to making things – I get it from Dad, Mum hasn't any patience with sewing. What's this I'm wishing? *That they could see my little shirts*? Unreal! A quick look down the slanted view at the garden where Mum is squatting on the lawn in the old lotus position with Doris prone. Obviously they're discussing me though I can't hear the words. That gives me a chance to do the talking: how different this could have been, dears, and don't blame me, it was you that made it impossible. But when I look again I see that Dad hasn't cut the grass and there are weeds in the flowerbeds. Cover the view quickly, concentrate on *what must be*, Dad at the golf club as usual and Mum selling her flags, and Chrissie and Pete on Sundays!

Archie took me out for the day on my birthday. We took the bike and rode into the country, and had a picnic in a field under some trees. We laughed because there had been sheep in that field and they had rubbed against the rough bark of the oaks, and left blobs of the natural undyed wool that Jelly was so patiently knitting. It smelt exactly the same. The meal was prawns, avocado pears, real mayonnaise out of a bottle and chocolate biscuits – all the things I like best, that he had taken the trouble to remember. Then unexpectedly he produced his accordion, which he had hidden at the bottom of the carrier, and a little self-consciously at first, played some cheerful tunes.

That was a climax of happiness, to sit comfortably propped against the sun-warmed oak, listening to Archie's French selection, watching his face, which was always animated but especially so when he played. There had been a sprinkling of rain in the night, just enough to wash the grass and bring out the smell of fields close-cropped in summer. There was a trail of pure white cloud across the sweet blue of the sky, and enough of a breeze to stir the leaves overhead. I was wearing his old sweater with my skirt and top, for it wasn't as warm as all that, and he had on a red plaid shirt and fawn cotton trousers. Anyone looking at us would have thought, an idyllic couple; and indeed it was true.

'Don't stop,' I said, when he had flourished to the end of 'La Vie en Rose'.

'What more do you want?'

'Anything you like!'

'Okay! Get ready to sing.'

Then he played the first line of 'Strawberry Fair'. 'Go on!' he said.

But now I had to shake my head. Suddenly I had to turn my face away, for this was Mum's tune in the old days. She used to sing it so often when I was small, and I still remembered the words. Dad liked it. But she hadn't sung for ages. What had happened, why had she stopped?

Oh, Archie was on dangerous ground with his folk tunes. So many of them roused these old memories. Mum and Dad had belonged to a folk club; now all that remained of that phase in their lives was her long hair. And suddenly I panicked – suppose Mum's cut her hair!

Archie saw that I was having thoughts, so he played a

jazzed-up version of 'Happy Birthday to You', and put what he called his 'squeeze box' away.

'Sorry,' he said. 'I've made you all nostalgic.'

'It doesn't matter. It's been a lovely day, a really lovely day.'

On the way home we saw a balloon race – the slowest thing in the world, the huge, differently coloured balloons strung out, apparently motionless, across the valley. We got off the bike and watched them. It was then that he said, and I think he had been wanting to say it for some time, and now it was possible because we were looking at the balloons and not at each other, 'Don't worry so much! Keep a good heart, and it'll come right, you know.'

'Will it?'

'Oh yes. Things do. People worry too much.'

So when I was in bed I didn't dial their number, I talked to Ann instead. We were trying to decide whether I was falling in love with Archie, which was bound to happen, as far as I could see, though 'falling in' is perhaps the wrong phrase – 'growing into' would be better. You can forget the surrogate father syndrome – there's nothing fatherly about Archie, who isn't as old as all that, and anyhow one Dad is enough for me. Tonight Ann said she would have to meet him before she could make a realistic contribution to the discussion, so the three of us went out for a Chinese meal, and while he and I talked, she observed us. (In my mind, of course. When I was lonely I acquired this habit of acting out little scenes and situations, my lips moved, which was disconcerting to others, etc. etc) When we were alone again (understand I still haven't moved from my bed in Archie's room), she said she thought we were in a suspended state of lovingness. This description made me smile and I was still smiling when I went to sleep.

Now the baby was close I cut down my hours at Gilda's, working at lunch time only. It was about a mile from the flat, and I walked there and back because Archie considered it health-giving. He had started buying me special foods, some of which were very expensive and disgusting, like ginseng tea. One day he came back with a book about natural childbirth and the unborn, heavily illustrated, which was also disgusting in places. Every day I passed the hospital where, unknown to the staff, I had decided to turn up when I went into labour. At that stage I reckoned they would have to take me in. Archie knew as little about it as I did, and he certainly never opened the childbirth book; when he saw that it lay about unread, he changed it for Oriental Flower Painting (conducive to elevated thought). He became anxious as August passed and I got very heavy, but I knew I was well, though my feet ached, and I could only move slowly. I was cheerful too. It had much cheered me, what he said about not worrying, and things coming right. In fact I hadn't bothered Mum lately; the barriers were still up but I hadn't needed to dwell on her unjustifiable attitudes and behaviour.

Bath was full of tourists, and Gilda's was busy. There was hardly room for me now in the slip of a kitchen with the microwave and the washing-up machine, and I was too big to fit between the tables. I wiped trays and made sandwiches. At three I left the place and hove down the street like a ship in full sail. I didn't mind being huge like this; it made sense of the months before, which were rolling up behind me like a scroll with the story of my child already started on it. That would be what he would bring into the world, his dowry so to speak. But he was very cumbersome in the heat. Archie would be speechless if he was twins.

I made it to the gap in the railings where Jellybean's gate should have hung, and stood there getting my breath for the last lap up the steps. Some people had little trees in tubs on their front paving, but we had a dustbin each (apart from Jelly, who disposed of her bottles in secret ways). It was bin day tomorrow and two were full of rubbish, spilling out under the lids; you could see that the chef ate Japanese and the schoolteachers read a lot of papers. The typists had recently departed, all together, so Jelly was in the middle of viewing new tenants and that bin was empty; while ours was only ever half-full, a sealed bag within, the lid firmly down. Archie had views about rubbish and he went for miles to recycle things. I stood looking, panting.

The rush of warm water down the insides of my legs was a shock. I scrambled myself together, tackled the steps still dripping, opened the door, took refuge. But you aren't due for a fortnight! What are you thinking about?

I stare at my face in Archie's gilt-edged mirror. I'm all lit up – pink cheeks, sparkling eyes. I haven't had my hair cut since I left home and it's grown down to my shoulders; it looks a bit lank, a bit sweaty. I find my shampoo and towel, and give it a quick wash. While I'm doing that, the baby unexpectedly gives a downward twist and I feel suddenly tight. It isn't a pain. I hold on to the washbasin. I let go and give my hair another rinse, wipe my face and rub my hair with the towel. I'm going back down the passage when – *this is a pain* – like a period pain but huge – stopping me – taking over – hills – mountains . . . . Familiar feet on the stairs, the voice of the Jellybean.

'Hallo, Liz! All right, dear?'

I focus in her direction – she isn't drunk, which could be a good thing. 'Yes, thanks.'

She observes me over the banisters. 'It's due any minute, isn't it?'

'That's right.'

'But I think they're often late.'

'Oh, I think so.'

'Good luck, anyway. Take care!' And *she goes out*. But, Jelly! I gape after her, suddenly filled with panic. Archie said he'd be late tonight. I find ten p, try him at the shop. No answer! No way now of getting hold of him! No help! Help!

I sit down in the window, get a grip on myself, rack my brains to remember the little I've read. Several hours it will take. Won't it? Here comes a pain – mounting – gathering me in to the last hair – gradually subsiding. Stories of Ann's colourful family, the cousin who had her baby in the phone booth while she was fumbling for change . . . . But if these are contractions they're coming fast, this could happen to me!

I'm shaking all over. I get up, put the kettle on, make myself a mug of good strong tea, stir in plenty of sugar. Oh Archie come. The room has gone grey like a prison.

Maybe they won't take me in at the hospital. Headline: Elizabeth Russell, alias Jenny alias Liz Davis, listed as a Missing Person in April, was found last night giving birth on the pavement. Mother and child are now in care.

Time passes – the pains go away. I feel unsettled, distressed, sick at the thought of food. I sit very still in the creaking cane chair in the window. My hands cover the baby, who has stopped moving. My stomach feels hard, like a fist.

The lamps go on in the street outside. They shine through the trees and cast a fitful orange light, a shifting pattern on the ceiling of the bay where I am sitting. I've never noticed this before. It seems the worst of omens.

A pain returns with more purpose, a rising tide that catches, holds, wrings. I heave off the chair, pace the room, glimpse my face in the glass – haggard, pale, full of dread. *This can't happen to me. I'm not going to be able to bear it.*

I open the trunk, get out the cherished packets, lay the little shirts on the bed, the tiny vests and boots, Jelly's patent suit always good for a grin for no way could it fit anything human, painfully completed with a purple bow – 'then it can be either, you see. You wouldn't want a boy in pink or a girl in blue.' I couldn't care less, it's odd that she does. *Oh Archie come.* I put my flannel and toothbrush into a bag, with one outfit for the baby, two sleeping shirts for myself, my hairbrush and towel. This part of me is on auto-pilot. For these pains – my own personal labour designed to wrench my baby out of my body – are coming every ten minutes. While my hands pack I hear the outside door – I stumble hastily to see who it is – oh be Archie –

Jelly in the hall

'Do you think you could get me a taxi?'

'Oh darling!' She looks furtive, backed against the pay phone, clutching her bottle-bulging bag. She leans forward, whispers with nightmare coyness, 'Is It on its way?'

'Yes.'

'Oh Liz! You poor love!'

She rings taxis, fumbling the coins into the slot, no answer, no answer. She sallies out Aunt Sally on the pavement to hail one God knows how long this will take

but I remember to collect my luggage, some money

help myself down the steps, rather jerky very trembly

an elderly taxi driver is having words with Jellybean. It seems he doesn't want to take me unless she comes too. It's happened to him before and he doesn't want to repeat the experience. So she sits beside me and holds my hand, which is kind but throws me. She insists on paying for the cab and I leave her arguing over the fare.

17

I give my particulars. (If you're brought in dying after a road accident, do they still ask for them? Name, date of birth, address, blood group if you know it, GP if any?) This time, apart from a massive pain when I grab the nurse and everything falls on the ground, I am easier in my mind: I am now sixteen and I have a right to leave home and there is nothing they can do about it. I still call myself Elizabeth Davis but my birth date is genuine, and I give Archie's address. I say I can't remember the name and address of my doctor and I haven't any next of kin.

'Not even your mum?'

'No.'

The nurse isn't much older than me. She says, 'No mum! That's a shame.'

Once I would have said, 'Is it?' in a cold tone.

The midwife examines me and I ask her how long it will be.

'Oh dear, I can't tell you yet. You're coming along nicely.'

'I mean as long as an hour? Longer than that?' I shall die, don't you realize? I can't stand much more of this. It's like being disembowelled again and again.

'Walk up and down if you find it helpful. We'll give you some pethidine when things really get going.'

My God!

Slow march up the corridor, clinging to the radiators; crawl down the corridor, clawing at the windowsill. A nurse comes out and puts her arm round me.

'Why not pop back to bed and try and get some rest?'

She has to be joking!

Blank white ceiling occasionally stroked by the light of a

passing car. In lucid moments, a consciousness of the hospital in night-time suspension around me. *Oh God I can't handle this and there is no way out oh Mum*

'Relax,' says the nurse. 'Try to relax.' But this is unforgivable this pain this is a screaming sin that women should suffer like this you did it twice so did little old Granny for you and your twin who died soon after *it's no picnic love* north country accent very wry

Mum why aren't you here with me why aren't you helping *Mum I wish you were here*

on a shot of pethidine the line between us opens and I see she has done up her hair with hospital bandages and is wearing a spotless white gown she keeps moving her lips but I can't hear what she says

sorry sorry sorry is all I have to say

'There's no need to apologize,' says the midwife bending over me so our bodies touch

asking am I getting little pushy pains dear

feet braced against two checked uniforms the urge to push is impossible irreversible this baby will shoot across the room pant pant pant they are saying into the tearing climax *crowned* I hear the word

crowned

this is my baby

the weight of a head in the crook of my arm

slow return to a functional room where people bear babies back to the banal the daily delivery

'Isn't he beautiful? What are you going to call him?'

'I haven't decided.'

18

It was a nice hospital, and kind in imaginative ways. They put me on my own in a side ward with the baby beside me in his cot, and I was particularly grateful for this at visiting times because nobody came to see me, and it would have been miserable in the maternity ward without any visitors or flowers. Now it didn't matter, I was only in five days, and I hadn't really expected Archie – I realized that hospital visiting certainly wasn't his thing. Jelly, on the other hand. . . .

I had the baby in bed with me a lot. He just fitted nicely between my hip and armpit, he was warm and pink with thin legs and tiny clutching hands. It's odd how a baby face can mirror a grown-up one – he had a definite look of Dad. Not the temper though, my boy – we'll put a stop to that! But I had plenty of milk and I fed him whenever he wanted, so that he shouldn't know what it was to cry. And I thought, I had many deep thoughts, about Archie and me, and Mum.

What's he like?

A, I admire him. B, he's busy – he never lounges about. C, he's careful about people, particularly me. So, naturally, D, he's dear to me. E, he's elegant, at least I think so. F, he's fantastical – I mean he doesn't behave like everyone else, which I like. G, he's good. I can't imagine that he would ever do a mean or selfish thing. No, probably not the sort of person you'd expect me to fall for, but then I've probably changed quite a lot. Maybe I never was exactly what you thought.

'So you're off home this morning. Is anyone coming to fetch you?'

'I thought I'd get a cab, it's only just up the road.'

'Fine, and then a midwife will look in tomorrow, okay? We like to keep an eye on you and the baby. She'll call every day to begin with.'

'Thanks very much.'

'Doesn't he look a poppet! You'll bring him back to see us, won't you? It's nice when the Mums keep in touch.'

'Of course I will.'

A maternity unit is like an oasis in a desert. You step out of the door and you feel threatened. You pull the blanket more closely round the baby's head, grip your little bag tightly, try to keep a sense of proportion; for you feel as if there are wild things round every corner, and you are horribly vulnerable.

It was only ten o'clock when I arrived. Jellybean's milk was standing at the top of the steps and I carried it in to the hall, for the sun was already warm. I went into our room. Archie wouldn't be home before five at the earliest. I had plenty of time to organize the baby, find something to eat, have a rest. I pushed back the blanket from his sleeping face, and looked round. His tiny clothes were still laid out on the bed. My dirty teacup was still under the chair.

Warning bells began beating in my brain. Had Archie been home? I wouldn't have believed it, except that a vase of red roses stood in the middle of the table. While I was staring about, I sensed rather than heard someone behind me, in the doorway.

It was Jelly. My immediate thought was that she must have been drinking a lot.

'Liz dear,' she said, unsteadily. Then in a different voice, 'Let's have a look at Baby.'

I opened out the blanket so she could see more of him. I didn't want her to hold him and she didn't try to.

'Well then,' she said. 'Isn't he perfect – it is a little boy, isn't it?'

I said it was. I was beginning to tremble, without knowing why. But she was so unlike herself.

'I have to tell you,' she said, and broke off. Then I saw to my horror that it wasn't alcohol, it was tears that had made her face sodden. Woe had ravaged her like drink.

'But Jelly—'

She waved me to silence. Her voice dropped to the throbbing tone. 'I have to tell you. I must and will. When he came back, and I told him you had gone into hospital, he went off again on his bike. And that was all I knew about it, until next day. A policeman called then you see, my dear.

'It seems he came to grief at the crossroads. No one will ever know for certain where he was going. But it must have been to see you, Liz, for he had this bunch of roses with him, that he must have gone down past the abbey to fetch, because nobody else stays open as late as that. He must have meant them for you.'

She said, 'Don't cry, my dear. They got me in to identify the body and there wasn't a mark on him. Believe me, to look at his face – you would have said he hadn't a care in the world.'

She brought me some food, and sat with me part of that day. We didn't talk about Archie, we didn't talk much at all. As she was leaving she said, 'I never asked what you are calling your baby.'

'I shall call him after Archie.'

'James Archer Davis.'

'No – Archer Russell.'

'That's nice. I like Russell – is that a family name?'

'Yes,' I said.

I didn't take out any of the books, or touch the clothes, or speak in my mind to Archie. After all, I knew well enough that what he loved most was freedom. It was for Jelly to pore over letters, old photographs, keep turning the knife in her heart. I was young enough to say goodbye.

I fed Archer, and while he was sleeping I went into the hall to phone. My hand pressing out the number wasn't quite steady.

'Hello – Mum? This is me speaking.'

Other great reads ❦ *from* **Red Fox**

Further Red Fox titles that you might enjoy reading are listed on the following pages. They are available in bookshops or they can be ordered directly from us.

If you would like to order books, please send this form and the money due to:

ARROW BOOKS, BOOKSERVICE BY POST, PO BOX 29, DOUGLAS, ISLE OF MAN, BRITISH ISLES. Please enclose a cheque or postal order made out to Arrow Books Ltd for the amount due, plus 30p per book for postage and packing to a maximum of £3.00, both for orders within the UK. For customers outside the UK, please allow 35p per book.

NAME _____

ADDRESS _____

_____

Please print clearly.

Whilst every effort is made to keep prices low, it is sometimes necessary to increase cover prices at short notice. If you are ordering books by post, to save delay it is advisable to phone to confirm the correct price. The number to ring is THE SALES DEPARTMENT 071 (if outside London) 973 9700.

Other great reads *from* **Red Fox**

The Maggie Series   Joan Lingard

MAGGIE 1: THE CLEARANCE

Sixteen-year-old Maggie McKinley's dreading the prospect of a whole summer with her granny in a remote Scottish glen. But the holiday begins to look more exciting when Maggie meets the Frasers. She soon becomes best friends with James and spends almost all her time with him. Which leads, indirectly, to a terrible accident . . .

ISBN 0 09 947730 0   £2.50

MAGGIE 2: THE RESETTLING

Maggie McKinley's family has been forced to move to a high rise flat and her mother is on the verge of a nervous breakdown. As her family begins to rely more heavily on her, Maggie finds less and less time for her schoolwork and her boyfriend James. The pressures mount and Maggie slowly realizes that she alone must control the direction of her life.

ISBN 0 09 949220 2   £2.50

MAGGIE 3: THE PILGRIMAGE

Maggie is now seventeen. Though a Glaswegian through and through, she is very much looking forward to a cycling holiday with her boyfriend James. But James begins to annoy Maggie and tensions mount. Then they meet two Canadian boys and Maggie finds she is strongly attracted to one of them.

ISBN 0 09 951190 8   £2.50

MAGGIE 4: THE REUNION

At eighteen, Maggie McKinley has been accepted for university and is preparing to face the world. On her first trip abroad, she flies to Canada to a summer au pair job and a reunion with Phil, the Canadian student she met the previous summer. But as usual in Maggie's life, events don't go quite as planned . . .

ISBN 0 09 951260 2   £2.50

Other great reads *from* **Red Fox**

Discover the great animal stories of Colin Dann

JUST NUFFIN

The Summer holidays loomed ahead with nothing to look forward to except one dreary week in a caravan with only Mum and Dad for company. Roger was sure he'd be bored.

But then Dad finds Nuffin: an abandoned puppy who's more a bundle of skin and bones than a dog. Roger's holiday is transformed and he and Nuffin are inseparable. But Dad is adamant that Nuffin must find a new home. Is there *any* way Roger can persuade him to change his mind?

ISBN 0 09 966900 5 £2.99

KING OF THE VAGABONDS

'You're very young,' Sammy's mother said, 'so heed my advice. Don't go into Quartermile Field.'

His mother and sister are happily domesticated but Sammy, the tabby cat, feels different. They are content with their lot, never wondering what lies beyond their immediate surroundings. But Sammy is burningly curious and his life seems full of mysteries. Who is his father? Where has he gone? And what is the mystery of Quartermile Field?

ISBN 0 09 957190 0 £2.50

Other great reads *from Red Fox*

THE WINTER VISITOR   Joan Lingard

Strangers didn't come to Nick Murray's home town in winter.
And they didn't lodge at his house. But Ed Black had—and Nick
Murray didn't like it.

Why had Ed come? The small Scottish seaside resort was
bleak, cold and grey at that time of year. The answer, Nick
begins to suspect, lies with his mother—was there some past
connection between her and Ed?

ISBN 0 09 938590 2   £1.99

STRANGERS IN THE HOUSE   Joan Lingard

Calum resents his mother remarrying. He doesn't want to move
to a flat in Edinburgh with a new father and a thirteen-year-old
stepsister. Stella, too, dreads the new marriage. Used to living
alone with her father she loathes the idea of sharing their small
flat.

Stella's and Calum's struggles to adapt to a new life, while
trying to cope with the problems of growing up are related with
great poignancy in a book which will be enjoyed by all older
readers.

ISBN 0 09 955020 2   £1.95

Other great reads *from* **Red Fox**

Fantasy fiction—the Song of the Lioness series

ALANNA—THE FIRST ADVENTURE
Tamora Pierce

Alanna has just one wish—to become a knight. Her twin brother, Thom, prefers magic and wants to be a great sorcerer. So they swop places and Alanna, dressed as a boy, sets off for the king's court. Becoming a knight is difficult—but Alanna is brave and determined to succeed. And her gift for magic is to prove essential to her survival . . .

ISBN 0 09 943560 8   £2.50

IN THE HAND OF THE GODDESS
Tamora Pierce

Alan of Trebond is the smallest but toughest of the squires at court. Only Prince Jonathan knows she is really a girl called Alanna.

As she prepares for her final training to become a knight, Alanna is troubled. Is she the only one to sense the evil in Duke Roger? Does no one realise what a threat his steely ambition poses?

Alanna must use every ounce of her warrior skills and her gift for magic if she is to survive her Ordeal of Knighthood—and outwit the dangerous sorcerer duke.

ISBN 0 09 955560 3   £2.50

The third and fourth titles in the Song of the Lioness series, THE GIRL WHO RODE LIKE A MAN and LIONESS RAMPANT will be published by Red Fox in July 1992.

Other great reads ✎ *from* **Red Fox**

**Haunting fiction for older readers from
Red Fox**

THE XANADU MANUSCRIPT
John Rowe Townsend

There is nothing unusual about visitors in Cambridge.

So what is it about three tall strangers which fills John with a mixture of curiosity and unease? Not only are they strikingly handsome but, for apparently educated people, they are oddly surprised and excited by normal, everyday events. And, as John pursues them, their mystery only seems to deepen.

Set against a background of an old university town, this powerfully compelling story is both utterly fantastic and oddly convincing.

'An author from whom much is expected and received.'
Economist

ISBN 0 09 9751801   £2.50

ONLOOKER   Roger Davenport

Peter has always enjoyed being in Culver Wood, and dismissed the tales of hauntings, witchcraft and superstitions associated with it. But when he starts having extraordinary visions that are somehow connected with the wood, and which become more real to him than his everyday life, he realizes that something is taking control of his mind in an inexplicable and frightening way.

Through his uneasy relationship with Isobel and her father, a Professor of Archaeology interested in excavating Culver Wood, Peter is led to the discovery of the wood's secret and his own terrifying part in it.

ISBN 0 09 9750708   £2.50

Other great reads from **Red Fox**

Enter the gripping world of the REDWALL saga

REDWALL   Brian Jacques

It is the start of the summer of the Late Rose. Redwall Abbey, the peaceful home of a community of mice, slumbers in the warmth of a summer afternoon. The mice are preparing for a great jubilee feast.

But not for long. Cluny is coming! The evil one-eyed rat warlord is advancing with his battle-scarred mob. And Cluny wants Redwall . . .

ISBN 0 09 951200 9   £3.50

MOSSFLOWER   Brian Jacques

One late autumn evening, Bella of Brockhall snuggled deep in her armchair and told a story . . .

This is the dramatic tale behind the bestselling *Redwall*. It is the gripping account of how Redwall Abbey was founded through the bravery of the legendary mouse Martin and his epic quest for Salmandastron. Once again, the forces of good and evil are at war in a stunning novel that will captivate readers of all ages.

ISBN 0 09 955400 3   £3.50

MATTIMEO   Brian Jacques

Slagar the fox is intent on revenge . . .

On bringing death and destruction to the inhabitants of Redwall Abbey, in particular to the fearless warrior mouse Matthias. Gathering his evil band around him, Slagar plots to strike at the heart of the Abbey. His cunning and cowardly plan is to steal the Redwall children—and Mattimeo, Matthias' son, is to be the biggest prize of all.

ISBN 0 09 967540 4   £3.50